Rewards for Kids!

Rewards for Kids!

READY-TO-USE

Charts &
Activities

FOR POSITIVE
PARENTING

Virginia M. Shiller, PhD

with Meg F. Schneider

Illustrated by Bonnie Matthews
based on original chart designs by Janet C. O'Flynn

American Psychological Association • Washington, DC

Published by
APA Life Tools
American Psychological Association
750 First Street, NE
Washington, DC 20002
www.apa.org

To order
APA Order Department
P.O. Box 92984
Washington, DC 20090-2984

Tel: (800) 374-2721; Direct: (202) 336-5510
Fax: (202) 336-5502; TDD/TTY: (202) 336-6123
Online: www.apa.org/books/
E-mail: order@apa.org

In the U.K., Europe, Africa, and the Middle East, copies may be ordered from
American Psychological Association
3 Henrietta Street
Covent Garden, London
WC2E 8LU England

Typeset in Sabon by Susan K. White, Burke, VA

Printer: Automated Graphic Systems, White Plains, MD
Book Designer: Susan K. White, Burke, VA
Technical/Production Editor: Kristen R. Sullivan

The opinions and statements published are the responsibility of the authors,
and such opinions and statements do not necessarily represent the policies of the
American Psychological Association.

Library of Congress Cataloging-in-Publication Data

Shiller, Virginia M. (Virginia Marie)
    Rewards for kids! : ready-to-use charts and activities for positive parenting /
    by Virginia M. Shiller with Meg F. Schneider ;
    illustrated by Bonnie Matthews based on original chart designs by Janet C. O'Flynn.
        p. cm.
    ISBN 1-59147-006-4 (alk. paper)
    1. Child rearing. 2. Parenting. 3. Reward (Psychology) in children.
    I. Schneider, Meg F. II. Matthews, Bonnie, 1963- III. Title.

HQ769.S5189 2003
649'.1--dc21   2002038312

British Library Cataloguing-in-Publication Data
A CIP record is available from the British Library.

Printed in the United States of America
First Edition

TO BEN,
DEREK,
AIDAN,
AND KATHLEEN

Contents

Part 3

Your Toolbox: Reward Charts and More 117

* These charts are larger and can be found folded in the very back of the book.

OUR STORY

Many years ago, when my son was in kindergarten, I had the good fortune to meet Janet O'Flynn, the mother of another kindergartener. Like my son, her child was strong-willed and often wished to march to the beat of his own drum. Janet and I quickly found we shared an interest in developing positive and creative ways for encouraging good behavior. Janet's talent for designing unique charts and reward activities fit well with my desire to find ways of engaging my children's interest. In between sorting out carpooling schedules, exchanging concerns about our sons' adjustment to a new school, and discussing the quirks of our younger children, Janet and I soon realized that our ideas and experience might be of value to other parents. We began to develop the beginnings of a book.

I can still remember the afternoon I sat down in Janet's kitchen and noticed the Feed the Kitty chart on her kitchen fridge. Janet's 3-year-old daughter had refused to drink the yucky pink stuff (antibiotics prescribed for an ear infection) until Janet sketched a cat that could be "fed" with food stickers each time her child took her medicine. "Neat idea! Let's put it in the book," was my immediate response.

The Dinosaur Land and Welcome to the Zoo charts were inspired by our children's fascination with animals. My preschooler finally began to cooperate with toothbrushing when I taped the Welcome to the Zoo chart on the wall beside his bed and offered him the opportunity to add to the animal collection each evening. The chart became a much-loved wall decoration and to this day accompanies our other favorite childhood memorabilia in safekeeping. A number of the sample plans, such as the one for toothbrushing, are based on actual plans we developed for our own children.

Clearly, this is not a book conceived in a psychology lab or professional discussion group. It is the work of two moms who sought to bring the knowledge of their professions (Janet worked as an occupational therapist and I as a clinical psychologist) to bear on the job of child rearing. Quite frankly, the excitement of developing a book also helped us remain upbeat about the challenges in facing the perils of parenting.

The book was put aside for a while as the pressures of work and home life limited time available to polish the manuscript and search for a publisher willing to consider a nontraditional type of book. The passage of time had an unexpected benefit, however. As the book approached publication, our children were nearing adulthood. I now have confirmation of what I argue in the text—that the appropriate use of rewards when children are young does not produce individuals who expect to be rewarded for every accomplishment! Janet and I are pleased to see that our children are pursuing their self-chosen goals without seeking external payoffs for their efforts. They have become eager to take on challenges and to make their own responsible contributions to their families and to the community.

When I have shared evolving versions of this book with others, I have been gratified to receive enthusiastic responses. Parents who have consulted with me in my private practice about challenges with their children have found the book a useful adjunct to counseling. Also, graduate students and interns I have supervised at the Yale Child Study Center have told me that the charts and reward activities are much more imaginative than others they encountered in their training.

The book came to full maturity when Meg Schneider joined the team. Meg is an accomplished writer with much experience in the mental health field. (And, I might add, she is also a parent of two!) Meg's delightful sense of humor, her down-to-earth writing style, and her clear vision of how to organize this kind of book helped transform my manuscript from a somewhat dry guidebook to a book inviting enough for weary parents to pick up after the children are finally tucked into bed. Meg not only brought to the project her skill in writing with clarity and wit but also contributed ideas for the Reward Plans that were based on strategies from her own work with children and families.

I do hope that this book will provide you with helpful guidance as you and your youngster confront a variety of challenges common to childhood. And I also hope that the knowledge that this book was developed by parents who, like you, have been there "in the trenches" will help you believe that you, too, can engage in positive parenting.

Finally, I would like to express appreciation for the creative ideas and for the supportive and helpful feedback I received from many individuals. A number of parents, grandparents, and child care professionals provided feedback about the manuscript and shared their personal experiences with using Reward Plans, including Beth Klingher, Ellen Brainard, Marjorie Orellana, Lauren Pinzka, Torr Hepburn, Robert Faulstich, Lisa Weiler, Linda Poland, David Roberts, Nancy Faulstich, Michael Dunn, Dorothy Bowe, and Alma Bair. My colleagues at the Yale Child Study Center have long provided inspiration and support, and I would in particular like to thank Drs. Sara Sparrow and Diane Findley and students Cheryl Klaiman, Arielle Berman, and Anna Cassar for their influence on this book. Other colleagues who were especially helpful were Ann Singer, Deborah Gruen, Karen Steinberg, Rosalind Atkins, Bonnie Becker, Nancy Lesh, and Joan Wexler. My development editor at the American Psychological Association, Judy Nemes, consistently provided gentle guidance and wisdom, and production editor Kristen Sullivan ably oversaw the completion of the book. And I owe a great debt of gratitude to my husband Bob as well as to Janet's husband Donnel for their ongoing and abundant enthusiasm for and encouragement of this project.

ABOUT THE AUTHOR

Virginia M. Shiller, PhD, is a licensed clinical psychologist specializing in child and family therapy. She completed a clinical fellowship in psychology at the Department of Psychiatry, Harvard Medical School and a postdoctoral fellowship at the Bush Center for Child Development and Social Policy, Yale University. She is currently a lecturer at the Yale Child Study Center and has a private practice.

Dr. Shiller actively promotes children's needs through writing as well as political advocacy. As chair of the Children and Youth Committee of the Connecticut Psychological Association, she received the association's 2002 Award for Extraordinary Service. Dr. Shiller is the proud parent of two sons and lives with her husband Robert in New Haven, Connecticut.

PART I

All About Reward Plans

"No, I Won't!"

INTRODUCTION

Julia could hear the birthday party still going on when she arrived to pick up Sally. For the briefest moment, she considered walking away. Anything to avoid the inevitable scene. But the choice wasn't hers. She had to grab her daughter and run—they were expected at a family dinner.

"Hello!" the birthday girl's mother, Anne, sang out as she opened the door. "We're just winding up. Sally had a wonderful time!" She turned to look for Sally. Spotting her, she called out, "Sally, honey, your mom is here!"

Sally looked up and took one look at Julia, and it was as if her face was cracking into a thousand pieces. "NOOOOOOOOOOO!" she howled as Julia stood there filled with the familiar mix of anger, embarrassment, and frustration she always felt when it was time to pick Sally up from a play date or party. Instantly, Julia started rummaging around in her shoulder bag for a distraction. Something. Anything to get Sally to chill out and leave. Julia's searching fingers touched the fur of a tiny stuffed animal she had picked up as a gift for her niece. She glanced at Sally, who was now clutching a table as if someone would have to pry her loose. This would do it, Julia thought to herself.

"Do what?" the question suddenly reverberated through her mind.

She offered the toy to Sally. *Julia shrugged. Who cared? What choice did she have?**

Actually, Julia does have a choice. She can choose to help both Sally and herself take control. Right now they are stuck in a maddening tango, and neither one knows how to turn off the music and step away.

I am a psychologist who specializes in working with children, and I have long been fascinated by the dynamics, both difficult and not, that characterize parent–child relationships. Once I became a parent, I grew particularly interested in the many ways parents and children wrestle with each other. And I sought to discover new ways for parents and children to move together in harmonious ways.

Thus the birth of *Rewards for Kids! Ready-to-Use Charts and Activities for Positive Parenting.* This book will explore one of the best ways I have found to change the music. Julia and Sally *can* find another dance that, during potentially difficult moments, has far less drama, a lot more warmth, and a much more positive ending.

Quite literally, there is a tyranny at work for Sally and Julia at pickup time. Sally is the tyrant now, demanding payment for behaviors that ought to come free. If Julia were to start nagging, screaming, punishing, threatening, or criticizing, they would merely switch roles. And in the end, both mother and child would end up frustrated, furious, and feeling misunderstood. If this process continues unchecked, Sally and perhaps even her mother may become frightened by their own inability to stay in control of their actions.

Certainly, as a parent, you've been here. You've experienced a time (probably many times) when your child was behaving in a way that you simply could not tolerate. Perhaps the behavior was embarrassing (using foul language), frightening (running out of sight at the playground), frustrating (refusing to get homework done on time), or simply annoying (whining the moment you hit the grocery store together). Whatever

---

**See the box at right for a Reward Plan that would work for Sally and her mother!*

The Party Departure Reward Plan for Sally and Her Mother

Imagine that you are Sally's mother, and you are facing yet another party. You cannot bear what happens when you arrive to pick her up, and so you devise a Reward Plan to help you both get through the departure.

Before Sally goes to her next party, you sit her down and commiserate. "It must be so hard to leave a fun party—even though you know it's over." This will help Sally feel understood but also remind her that she isn't missing much when she goes. You deepen this experience for her by saying, "But I have a fun plan that I think will make it easier for you to go."

Sally may look at you warily at first, but just keep talking. "First of all, I think it will be easier if I call ahead before I leave the house. That way you'll know I'm on my way, you still have time to play, and you can keep in mind you will be leaving soon. You won't be surprised when I ring the doorbell. Then, when I come to the door, I'll give you 3 minutes to finish up what you're doing before you leave with me. You can remind me, too. You can say, 'Mom, 3 minutes!'"

Sally starts to smile. She likes that you're giving her some control.

Now you get to the reward part.

"Then, when you get into the car, I'm going to hand you something called a Prize Coupon *(for blank ones, see the Pull-Out section at the back of the book).* There will be crayons in the car, and you can color it however you please."

"What's that?" Sally asks. "Coupons?"

"Remember in the grocery store, when I had a coupon that gave me two boxes of cereal for the price of one? Your coupon will give you a chance to play one round of a board game with me tonight. When you're ready, you just walk over to me and hand me the coupon. You can say, "Mom, I claim my reward."

"Really?" Sally giggles. "I get to be the boss?"

You smile. "You get to receive a reward because you behaved well and like a big girl when I came to take you home."

You then show her what a Prize Coupon looks like, having already cut one out from this book. You place it in an envelope marked "Welcome Back From the Party!" You read the words to her with great enthusiasm.

"OK!" Sally says, reaching for the coupon. "Can I color the envelope now?"

the details, chances are that during those times you've felt desperate to find a way to escape from the problem. To just get on with the task at hand. *To get the job done.*

And yet you probably found your options limited. Resorting to punishment or threats left you and your child feeling alienated and miserable. So before you knew it, you may have been thinking, What wampum bead can I use? What carrot will do the trick? Yet when trying to find a positive incentive, you were plagued by the idea that you were doing something wrong. That you were *buying* good behavior and not teaching your child anything. That you were *bribing* your child to do something he ought to have been doing without any real protest at all.

Well, chances are you were. Join the club. It's a huge one.

But that was the past. You haven't etched anything in stone and, in fact, have every opportunity in front of you to creatively, positively, and even with good will and humor put a stop to those endless battles when only the threat of losing something or the impulsive promise of a new action figure, CD, or ice cream sundae subdues the fire. (By the way, when you do offer these kinds of bribes, you're most likely only temporarily postponing a battle with your child.)

FINDING A BETTER WAY

A Reward Plan is an extremely useful, enjoyable, and creative way to help your child improve her behaviors and to help both of you lay claim to some control over what happens next. Most important, a Reward Plan is a way to help your child break contrary patterns and move, by her own choice, toward productive behaviors that feel good. The plan is based on what is known as *behavior modification*, which is a fancy way to describe, for our purposes, what's happening when a child receives stars, stickers, points, or other tangible rewards directly after performing a desirable behavior. Your child is learning to associate good behavior with a rewarding outcome.

You may already be somewhat familiar with this principle. Many parents have used stars, candy, and more when encouraging their children through toilet training. Often the results are wonderful—and quick. Parents have intuitively known that simply explaining the benefits of using a toilet is not quite enough to get some children to eschew diapers. The truth is, the use of rewards frequently succeeds in changing behaviors when other techniques have failed.

Parents who have used a Reward Plan to toilet train their children rarely consider using similar plans for other problem behaviors that emerge over the years. But the benefits of rewards can be extended to a wide range of challenges. From about age 3, when children first become sophisticated enough to understand the requirements of a Reward Plan, through age 10 or so, most children are highly responsive to Reward Plans.

The basics of developing Reward Plans are quite simple. After thinking about the specific behaviors you would like to help your child to change, you decide on a realistic timetable for improving the behaviors. Then, you select a chart from Part 3 of this book so that you have a concrete, visual record for you and your child of his progress. You decide on an end-of-plan reward or a few possible rewards your child can choose from, sit down with your child, and introduce the plan in a positive manner. Finally, you consistently and encouragingly keep track of his success in meeting the plan requirements. (These steps will be discussed in more detail later.)

Of course, you may be concerned about using rewards in a broad range of circumstances, and perhaps you are already thinking, "My child is not a robot. What about how she feels?" "Shouldn't my child be good because I tell him to?" "Isn't a reward an awful lot like bribery?" or "What's to stop my child from requesting her own TV in return for regularly neatening her closet?" These are valid concerns that I believe I can easily relieve, but before I do so I think it would be helpful to look at the theoretical framework on which this plan is based. It will go a long way toward familiarizing you with the highly effective backbone of Reward Plans.

REWARDS: A CHECKERED HISTORY

Perhaps you've heard of behaviorism. It was a prominent movement in psychology during the first half of the 20th century, and in fact it is still very much alive. It's based on the principle that the behaviors of all creatures are governed by consequences. From mice to pigeons to dolphins to human beings, we are all more likely to do something if in the past it has resulted in a reward. Likewise, if a consequence is unpleasant, we are apt to avoid any future behavior that might get the same results.

For the most part, I agree with this construct. But at a certain point, strict behaviorism and I part company.

B. F. Skinner is the best-known behavioral psychologist. He began his career in a laboratory studying how to train rats and pigeons. He actually managed to teach pigeons to bat Ping-Pong balls by rewarding them with food! After using animals to work out the most expedient way of giving rewards to encourage learning (when to give them, how often, and over how long a period of time), he turned his attention to human beings. Skinner strongly believed that positive reinforcement would be as effective in child rearing as it was in animal training. Furthermore, he believed that what goes on in people's minds and with their emotions is irrelevant to understanding behavior. Children learn to eat their vegetables if they get dessert. Period. He made, in other words, a huge leap from rats and pigeons to children. Skinner designed a system for child rearing that paid complete attention to changing behaviors but showed little or no regard for the effects people's thoughts and feelings have on their actions.

Rest assured, I don't buy that. Not at all. I quite agree with parents who mistrust a system that diminishes their children's individuality and fails to respect their hearts and minds. I disagree that it does-n't matter what goes on internally as long as children learn to do as they are told. I don't like the idea of ignoring the fact that people are different from animals. Our children are thinking, feeling beings who experience the world in far more complex ways than simply, "If I do this, then I'll get that." There are quite frequently underlying factors contributing to problem behaviors that strict behaviorism cannot address. As a therapist, I believe mightily in seeking to understand the roots of fears and other difficult emotions.

In addition, I have always found the language of behaviorism too cold and mechanical. *Schedules and patterns of reinforcement, extinction of behaviors, stimulus generalization*—I do not relish using these phrases as a psychologist or a parent when contemplating how to understand and change a child's behaviors.

However, my opposition to a behavioral approach stops here. In fact, I have become a proponent of some of its principles, especially (yes, I admit it) after becoming a parent! I believe that the behavioral principle of rewarding good behavior, when combined with more analytical approaches to understanding the deeper causes of particular behaviors, can be highly effective in reaping dramatic short- and long-term changes.

Reward Plans should certainly not be the only parenting tool you use. A parent must always work to see when problem behavior is the result of hidden fear, hurt, anger, or frustration. Our children *need* to be understood. But there are times when love, empathy, and open communication just don't work alone. Children can find themselves trapped in patterns of behavior they cannot break—even once their feelings are understood. They often need us to help motivate them to move past ingrained contrary behaviors.

If your 9-year-old son is chronically coming home from school irritable and unhappy, resulting in a ritual fight match with his younger brother, you would be wise to talk to the teacher to see if he is being victimized at school or experiencing academic problems about which you have not yet been informed. You might also want to gently talk with him to see if he is able to tell you what's going on. But at the same time, for the sake of helping him get his aggression under control, securing the safety of his brother, and estab-lishing peace in the house, setting in motion a Reward Plan might quickly decrease the battles. It's amazing what a chart that tracks progress toward goals (such as no fights for an hour, morning, or day) can do!

Still, you might ask, are rewards *really* necessary? Doesn't my child, in the end, *want* to be good? That's an interesting question and one that needs to be examined, if for no other reason than to increase your understanding of, and thus patience with, your child's often seemingly intolerable behavior.

WHY CHILDREN FAIL TO BEHAVE WELL

Your child's innate desire to be good is often eclipsed by her own strong drive to become independent. Parents of 2-year-olds generally expect and tolerate the behavior that stems from this drive. But somehow, when it comes to older children, we have a harder time accepting rebelliousness and assertiveness. After all, now we can reason with our child. Shouldn't he just understand when we say, "You need to do this"? Well, he may understand on some level, but his drive for independence is still there. In fact, it's growing at such a clip that your logic and desires simply don't matter that much. "I want to be me!" is his almost unalterable stance.

Of course, children also have a desire to please their parents and to be loved by them. Thankfully, your child will often want to conform to your wishes to please you. But other times the push for independence will be so powerful that she might resist your requests simply to achieve a sense of control. "I say what I will do. I am the captain of my own ship!" she might be proclaiming through her noncomforming behaviors.

But there are other simple reasons why your children might resist behaving the way you would like. Good behavior generally requires more effort than bad, let's face it. Cleaning up a room just isn't as much fun as creating a mess. Good behavior also necessitates impulse control. It's a lot more appealing to grab four cookies than two!

Finally, it takes a while for children to have sufficient life experience to realize that positive behavior actually rakes in a lot more good fortune than obstreperous or negative behavior. It's much easier to assume that Mom's rules are just a nonsensical pain. But an unbridled passion for candy may begin to lessen after your child has had a few cavities. Suddenly he will want to pick up the toothbrush that has been resting idly in the medicine cabinet, just to avoid a visit to the dentist. Gradually, your child will learn that there is actually solid reasoning behind your expectations.

Notice here that I am talking about rewards you do not give. These are rewards your child begins to understand and work for, motivated by her own desire to feel good. That is ideally what will happen once you put the Reward Plan into place. Sometimes, for your child to discover the invisible and automatic rewards inherent in using positive behaviors, you have to create a happy result that he can readily anticipate, envision, and choose to work toward. Once there, the invisible rewards will be a kind of icing on the cake. Then after some time these rewards become, themselves, the cake.

And as for our children being the captain of their own ships—they will learn they still can be, only now it's in calmer waters. A Reward Plan is a wonderful way to help your child see the true benefits of great behavior.

So let's now take a look at how the plan works.

REWARD PLAN PRINCIPLES

First, a story.

"Tyler, would you please use your knife and fork!" Marion chided her 7-year-old son for the umpteenth time. "We do not live in a barn."

Tyler nodded, picked up his fork, skewered the chicken breast in its center, and brought the entire piece of meat to his mouth. As Marion watched mesmerized, he took one bite from the right side, then another from the left. It was clear from the gleam in his eye that Tyler knew something was wrong with this method, but his own sense of cleverness made it too delightful to stop.

After a few moments of silence (and after gathering herself), Marion smiled and said, "Well, this has got to stop." Actually, she'd been waiting for a moment like this.

Tyler grinned and continued to eat in a manner reminiscent of both Peter Pan and Henry VIII. Maybe it did have to stop, but not now. That was for sure.

"You know, Tyler, if you don't learn how to eat with some manners, no one is going to want to have a meal with you. Not me, not your dad, not your friends, and certainly not their parents," Marion sighed. "Good-bye sleepover invitations."

Marion wasn't sure, but it appeared that Tyler's grin suddenly shone a little less brightly. She immediately grew more sympathetic. "Tyler, I know you're able to eat with your knife and fork. I've seen you do it. I realize that when you're hungry, it seems like a terrible bother. But with a little practice, I think it will get easier. And people will think you're so grown-up!"

Eating with Silverware

	SAT	SUN	MON	TUES	WED	THURS	FRI	
Week 1	X	X	X	X				Out to Dinner
Week 2								Bake Cookies
Week 3								Ice Cream Sundae

Design-Your-Own Chart

Design-Your-Own Chart

Tyler shrugged. "I don't care," he said. "What's the big deal?" Marion noticed he was now slipping what was left of the chicken breast onto his plate and fingering the knife.

"So here's what we're going to do," Marion went on.

She went into the other room and returned with a brightly colored calendar chart that covered 3 weeks (for a blank one, see the Pull-Out section at the back of the book). At the top was a photo of Tyler at a Thanksgiving dinner, looking at the camera with fork in hand.

"Hey!" Tyler chuckled. "Where'd you get that?"

"I made it. The picture is from the family photo album," Marion replied. "So, each evening that you use your silverware, we'll put an X in a box on this chart. If you work at this all week and fill the chart with seven Xs, we'll go out to dinner on Saturday evening. You get to choose the restaurant! If you manage to do the same the second week, as a reward you and I can bake cookies together. And after the last week, you can earn an ice cream sundae with all the extras!"

Tyler's face lit up when he heard the list of rewards. But he wasn't going to give in easily. "Every night?" Tyler challenged. "What if we have pizza?"

Marion nodded. "Of course, you're right. Once a week you'll have a break when we eat pizza. And to make it even easier for you, every evening there will be one item on your plate you can eat with your fingers." She laughed. "I know your fingers are happiest when they're sticky."

Tyler looked down at his fingers, not at all sure if he was ready to smile. Marion cheerfully hung the chart by the kitchen table.

The next evening Tyler reluctantly sat down for dinner. Cleverly, Marion had prepared meat loaf entrée and mashed potatoes, which could be handled very easily using only a fork. An X appeared on the chart, no problem. The next evening she served London broil, which did require a fork and knife. Tyler handled them a little clumsily, accepted some of her help, sawed away *at the meat with exasperation, but received an X again because he had given it a significant try.*

Each evening, Tyler seemed a little more comfortable manipulating his utensils, and by the end of the week, he actually managed to cut the meat off a chicken breast just like the one he had eaten last week as if it were a roasted marshmallow at the end of a stick.

On Saturday, Tyler debated between a few restaurants and eventually settled on the local movie-themed bistro, which featured fun mirrors and arcade games. At the end of the second week, he and his mother baked enough cookies for him to treat his class. And by the conclusion of the third week, Tyler reached for his fork almost as naturally as he handled the controller for his video game . . . but not before he finished his banana split.

And it almost seemed to Marion that Tyler was starting to dislike the feeling of sticky fingers!

Marion, in this story, paid careful attention to the three most salient principles of any Reward Plan. She was

1. positive,
2. consistent, and
3. realistic.

As a result, Tyler was able to quickly follow along, see the benefits of doing so, and also experience his mother's flexibility—a relationship-boosting perk. He did not have to waste energy rigidly refusing to use his knife and fork because she made it so easy to cooperate.

★ BE POSITIVE ★

In study after study, psychologists have shown that positive incentives can be extremely effective in bringing about changes in behavior. And they've clearly demonstrated how a steady diet of criticism, negative comments, and punishment can take a toll on children's self-esteem and turn children off to any lessons parents are trying to convey. Simply put, positive outcomes are far more inspiring.

In a Reward Plan, parents can easily develop a strategy to emphasize the positive, and such a plan does allow parents the option both to award points or stickers for good behavior and to give negative marks

for poor behavior. But, keeping the focus on positive behaviors offers many benefits to both parents and children. Marion was positive in that she emphasized her confidence in Tyler's ability to eat with his silverware. She emphasized the benefits to Tyler of learning to eat in a "grown-up" way. The rewards she offered were sufficiently attractive to Tyler to gain his interest. And throughout the process, Marion conveyed a sense of impending pleasure!

★ BE CONSISTENT ★

Being consistent in reinforcing good behavior is critical to the success of a Reward Plan. And developing a system that reminds you and your child to be consistent is part of what the Reward Plan is all about. When you sit down with your child to design the plan and then hang up a reward chart in a central location, both you and your child are developing the motivation to pay close attention to the behaviors that need changing. After that, your child will follow along if she is sure that you are keeping track and that you are going to uphold your side of the bargain. Otherwise, she will lose her motivation to participate. After all, she hasn't yet experienced the invisible pleasures I spoke of earlier, and the more attainable ones will seem less and less bright if she cannot see her good behavior bearing fruit.

Marion religiously placed an X under each day that Tyler used his silverware at dinner. She hesitated only if he forgot and started to return to his old habits. In that case, she would repeat the rules. Each time, seeing that she was being consistent and "meant business," Tyler became more and more focused. He enjoyed the pleasure of receiving the X each time he used his utensils properly. The precious rewards were drawing nearer, as he knew they would, as long as he kept eating properly.

★ BE REALISTIC ★

Setting goals that are realistic and attainable is the third critical principle in any Reward Plan. Expecting too huge a change too quickly could overwhelm your child and actually bring on more negative behavior as he watches the goal swirl down the drain. You should be sure that the goals you set for good behavior are comfortably demanding and allow for success if your child puts forth a reasonable degree of effort.

Marion was very realistic. She focused only on Tyler's use of utensils and did not try to change any other bad habits. Although Tyler's behavior could stand improving in other areas, Marion recognized that her son needed to confront one challenge at a time. Successful manipulation of knife and fork at dinner was effort enough for a 7-year-old. Tyler could keep his mind on the rewards because, in truth, the behavior he had to produce was doable!

And then, of course, the ultimate goal was achieved. The invisible goal. Tyler discovered he actually enjoyed the feeling of having clean fingers!

Now, the three principles of being positive, consistent, and realistic come straight from the science of behaviorism. But I believe that there are two more principles that, if followed, can ensure that the Reward Plan is successful and fun. So let's look at the importance of being *caring* and *creative*.

★ BE CARING ★

I noted earlier that I part company with strict behaviorism because I think it ignores a person's inner life. What is happening for someone emotionally that is causing a particular behavior to surface? Many of the Reward Plans this book presents do not address behaviors involving any serious underlying unhappiness, frustration, or anxiety. Tyler, for instance, was simply a hungry 7-year-old who saw no purpose in the arduous task of cutting meat with knife and fork. Still, he had feelings about the step toward more civilized behavior that was being asked of him. His mother offered sympathy and support for the effort needed in learning to manipulate utensils.

There are, of course, other times when a behavior indicates that something more important might be going on inside a child. If you are seeing negative behaviors such as aggressive behavior, excessive clinging, incomplete homework, rudeness, and bedtime troubles, engage your child in a conversation about her thoughts and feelings *before* you put a Reward Plan into action.

If Tyler had begun to battle his mother whenever she suggested any change in his behavior, she would want to find out what was provoking so much rebelliousness. Why would he begin to fight with his mother over coming to dinner on time, sitting down to do his homework, or even going out to a restaurant? Addressing any underlying problems is critical not just for improving your child's emotional and physical health but also as the first step to helping him get back on track with the help of a Reward Plan.

★ BE CREATIVE ★

Once you get your child's interest by offering a reward, you can propose extras that will add zest to your plan and reinforce the lessons you want to teach. Marion, for example, used her creativity in attaching a photo to her chart that showed Tyler using a fork at Thanksgiving dinner; photos help your child feel this is "my" plan. In addition, your child can help design and decorate the chart. And after you get your child motivated, you can teach and reinforce new behaviors by doing things such as introducing role playing games. Throughout this book, you'll find lots of creative strategies for helping children learn and master new behaviors.

TAKING NEW BEHAVIORS OUT INTO THE WORLD

The story of Marion and Tyler is a fairly simple example of how the Reward Plan can work. But things often are more complicated. For instance, when the behavior you are trying to change occurs outside the home or involves people other than family members, you will have to deal with many more distractions, and rewards may have to be put off just a little while.

Consider a problem common to many parents who must bring a child along on the weekly grocery shopping trip.

Lauren's dad Roger had had it. He needed to do the weekly grocery shopping, and he had to take her with him. This was a given. Unfortunately, so were Lauren's histrionics. They would begin in aisle 1, when she started asking for cookies in a gnawing whine. If she wasn't given one within about a minute, her voice went up a few decibels and the editorials began.

"I want a cookie," she announced, as if no one knew this. "I hate it here. It smells bad." Sometimes she added sound effects. "BLECCHHHH!"

"Come, now," Roger would say, "We'll do this quickly. In and out." He would offer her nothing. Other times, he ignored her behavior. Then there was the threat of no TV. On many shopping trips Lauren ended up clutching exactly the cookie boxes she wanted, but the whining continued. By the time they made it out of the store, Roger and Lauren were exhausted and irritable. He vowed, "That's it. Never again"—which lasted until the next week, when the cupboards were once again bare.

What's going on here, besides the obvious fact that Lauren consistently creates an unbearable fuss when the two of them make their trip to the grocery store? Well, the answer includes a few things:

- Roger has not yet thought through, in advance, a plan that incorporates changes in both his own and Lauren's behaviors.
- He responds inconsistently.
- Most everything he does is negative. Ignoring her, issuing threats, and even the cookie box "fix" are signals of his frustration and anger.
- When he does give in, Roger is essentially rewarding Lauren's whining and obstreperous behaviors. If she wants attention, she's got it!

The first thing Roger must do is to decide exactly what behaviors he is aiming to change and how he will make these changes happen. Bringing positiveness, consistency, and realism into the picture is essential. He decides that he would like to accomplish two goals:

1. Lauren has to stop whining. She needs to speak normally and respectfully to him and to others.

2. Lauren has to entertain herself. She has to realize this is not "her" time. If Lauren does this, she can earn the privilege to ask to purchase two items.

Realizing that Lauren views the shopping trip as an endless trek, Roger begins to brainstorm about how to make the hour or so pass more easily for her. He develops a plan that is effective, that he can stick to, and that demands no more than Lauren can be expected to give.

★ DAD GETS POSITIVE ★

Roger tells Lauren that he knows shopping trips aren't fun for her, but that he thinks he has a plan for making it more interesting. He doesn't mention her poor behavior. In fact, he extends empathy: "Shopping is so boring for you!" he acknowledges, with heartfelt expression in his voice. He also tells her that he knows how good she is at acting like a big girl and promptly plays a game in which she says the same thing once as a little girl, and then again as an older child. Lauren enjoys showing off that she knows the difference.

★ DAD GETS CONSISTENT ★

Roger decides to divide up the grocery store trip by aisle and to reward Lauren with one Ticket (see the Pull-Out section at the back of the book) after she successfully makes it down the aisle without complaining. If after five aisles she earns four Tickets, she can request whatever box of cookies she would like. At the end of the 10 aisles, if she has earned another four Tickets, she can make another selection. Lauren's father hands her a "Ticket pouch" (a small bag into which Lauren can tuck her tickets). He allows extra time to periodically stop briefly so that Lauren can count up her Tickets. Roger is religious about giving her a Ticket whenever she earns it.

★ DAD GETS REALISTIC ★

Roger also turns his attention to strategies for avoiding boredom. He explains to Lauren, "It's hard doing things you don't really like to do, so it's a great idea to think of something to do that will keep you happy!" First he suggests she bring a storybook, but Lauren decides to carry her favorite doll and to discuss the grocery list with her. (Lauren is allowed to complain to her doll, but quietly!)

The outcome is a positive one. Lauren is motivated to change her behaviors. With an occasional reminder and some encouragement from her father, Lauren earns the eight tickets she needs to obtain both rewards! In the process, she learns some strategies for self-entertainment that will be useful to her throughout her life. By the third trip, Lauren collects all 10 Tickets. Despite the fact that there is no extra reward for earning every single possible Ticket, Lauren is beginning to pride herself on her maturity and self-control.

After about a month she grows bored of the system, and a few of her behaviors, in a very muted fashion, reappear. Roger changes the reward; he suggests that a card game of Go Fish when they get home might be a nice reward for good behavior. It's Lauren's favorite game. Her annoying behaviors fade away, and after a few weeks, Lauren forgets to request the game. She just goes to the store, doll in tow, and now knows from the start what two items she will request.

A WORD ABOUT PRAISE

A successful Reward Plan certainly shouldn't rely only on the delivery of rewards such as stickers, activities, or some desired object. Your praise for good behavior is a powerful part of a behavior plan. An appreciative smile in combination with generous compliments become a force that will help maintain behavioral changes after the excitement of other rewards is forgotten.

The fact is, a child's self-image is formed in large part by his perception of how his parents view him. A child secure in this self-image tends to be well behaved, as she not only anticipates that she will be successful when trying to be good but also expects the clear approval of others as an incentive.

Of course, when praising your child, you must be sure your words are believable. Overdoing it—"Wow! You are the best brother in the whole world!" in response to your son's ability *not* to hit his sister for one day can be counterproductive. There's no place to go from there, and besides, it sends the wrong message: Being the best brother requires a lot more than self-restraint!

However, despite praise's power, there are two groups of children for whom praise is not helpful. First, some children have a strong need to oppose their parents' wishes simply for the sake of asserting their own will. It is often best with these children to quietly mark the days of the Reward Plan in whatever way you have agreed on and then, with a quiet "congratulations," offer the reward. In other words, you will want to underplay the fact that the plan "worked" and that your child did what you wanted her to do.

The second group of children for whom praise is problematic have a rather pessimistic or negative view of themselves. If your son views himself as dumb or untalented, he might view your praise as phony and simply designed to buck him up. With such a child, you would do well to keep your comments specific and factual. "I see you got all of your homework done on time this week. That's five stars in a row. OK!" A gentle encouragement such as "I'm glad you kept it up. Hope you feel good about it too" will also suffice. In time, as your child experiences more success, he is likely to be more receptive to your praise. He might just think he deserves the compliment!

SHAPING: A SPECIAL APPROACH

Sometimes the behavior you may be seeking to change is so habitual (for example, getting out of bed in the middle of the night and climbing into yours) or broad based (such as general unpleasantness toward a younger sibling) that going from point A to point Z in one straight line simply cannot be done. Using the shaping technique, you reward a succession of behaviors that increasingly resemble the desired one.

Actually, B. F. Skinner did some interesting work with this approach. He found that pigeons could be taught to peck at a disk on the wall of their cage by rewarding them whenever they moved closer to the disk during a period of random pecking. Then, as they began to purposefully move closer, they were no longer rewarded for pecking at a distance but only for pecking closer still. Eventually, the pigeons were rewarded only when they actually pecked at the disk.

Of course, your children aren't birds, and they have far more going on in their heads than the pigeons in Skinner's experiments! You should certainly find out whether the child who climbs into your bed does because he is afraid or because something is going on between him and a sibling that needs exploring and intervention of another kind. Often, more complex and therefore difficult-to-eradicate behaviors require a multifaceted approach. But assuming you've started looking in an empathic way at what else is going on, and you're still left with a behavior that needs changing, a good way to proceed may be through shaping.

If, for example, you want to encourage your daughter to be kinder to her brother, you could begin by rewarding any behavior, even if accidental, that could be interpreted as kindness. Perhaps your daughter doesn't want to share a toy but offers a less desirable one to her brother instead, and her brother accepts it. "Great!" you might exclaim. "Wasn't that nice of you to give that toy to your brother! See how much he likes it?"

Although the praise may be largely undeserved, your daughter would most likely accept it and have an opportunity to experience the kind of attention she would receive if she indeed did act kindly toward her brother. With this encouragement, your daughter would probably begin to show more benevolence, and you could be more selective as to what behavior deserved a reward.

Shaping is also highly useful in teaching good manners. Your 8-year-old son may have a habit of finishing his meal, pushing his chair back from the table, and simply departing. If ultimately you want your son to say, "May I be excused?" when he leaves the dinner table, you could initially reward him for saying "Can I go now?" or "I'm leaving, OK?" The first step for your child is to remember and accept the idea that he should say something before leaving the table. Later, after the idea of saying something polite has taken hold, and your child is rather enjoying his reward, he might be more inclined to remember the most civilized way of asking to be excused.

IF, WHEN, AND HOW TO USE PUNISHMENT

There is one last piece to Reward Plans that I have hardly mentioned, largely because I see it as something to use only when necessary. Back to B. F. Skinner. It was his observation that positive reinforcement was extremely effective in changing behavior and his philosophical belief that people were more likely to choose the preferred road if a reward lay ahead and not the fear of punishment.

Loosely translated, children find more energy to do what you desire if doing so brings a positive outcome (a reward). A punishment in response to not doing what is expected in many cases serves merely as a deterrent. It may even inspire other problematic behaviors that stem from resentment and frustration. And it does nothing to enhance self-esteem.

However, studies have shown that including mild negative consequences in addition to positive incentives can help change behaviors more quickly. This may be important when children are doing something that hurts others or endangers themselves. On the other hand, if it is just, for instance, a missed chore or failure to practice the piano, you might do well to wait and see if the rewards are sufficient enticement for change. Again, putting more emphasis on the rewards instead of the consequences will infuse the Reward Plan with a spirit of good will.

Ebony's mom Chantal wanted her to stop hurting the cat by pulling his tail and squeezing him too hard. But Ebony kept forgetting. Chantal offered Ebony the chance to earn points if she stroked the cat gently, and if Ebony earned enough points in 2 weeks Chantal would take her and a friend to the movies. However, if Ebony hurt the cat, she would receive an "I Made a Mistake!" Slip (see the Pull-Out section at the back of the book). With each Mistake Slip, Ebony would lose a half hour of TV at night. Mom said encouragingly, "I bet you can learn to do gentle things with the cat so you can keep your TV shows and we can be off to the movies in 2 weeks!"

There are two ways to design a plan that incorporates a penalty. First, you can design a plan where a reward hinges on earning a specified number of check marks, points, tickets, or stars and not getting any more than a certain number of negative marks.

Maria had to stop pushing around her younger sister Nina. Maria's mom Susanna chose the Keeping Track chart (for a blank one, see the Pull-Out section at the back of the book) and told Maria she would receive a check mark for each day over 2 weeks that she used words and not her hands to relate to Nina and an X on each day she forgot and pushed. If she earned at least 11 check marks, she could have a sleepover party with three friends. If Maria earned more than three Xs, however, she would not earn the sleepover

this time. (But if Maria did not earn the sleepover, she probably would need Susanna's sympathy as well as encouragement so that next time around the goal would be attainable. Perhaps Susanna would need to spend some time talking about Maria's feelings of resentment for her sister. Also, she might help Maria figure out some strategies to avoid the urge to push.)

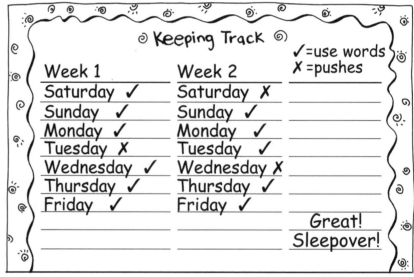

Keeping Track Chart

The second way to incorporate penalties into a Reward Plan is to tally points in two rows or columns, where one row marks steps toward a reward and the other indicates that your child is heading for a consequence. Fourteen stickers might mean your child gets to bake a cake. Every three Xs might mean your child has to have a time-out. With this approach, your child will be assured of earning his reward if he puts some effort into the plan. This method of incorporating a penalty may be the best choice if you think your child would become too upset if he failed to meet the reward goal first time around. Time-outs (or other penalties such as missing a television show or having to do an extra chore) given on the way to earning the reward would provide a warning to stop misbehavior. Depending on your child's age and personality, you could choose the Keeping Track chart or the Design-Your-Own chart to keep track of points gained and lost. An illustration of the Design-Your-Own chart used this way is on p. 122 in Part 3.

I do want to stress that it is important, if you are going to choose to combine rewards with penalties, to keep the tone as positive and understanding as possible. Again, keeping your eye on the rewards instead of the negative consequences will infuse the Reward Plan with a spirit of good will. Here are a few suggestions:

- When you design a chart with columns for positive and negative marks, you might want to label the two columns something like "Great Work!" and "Oops!" The latter indicates that you understand it was a mess up and that your child can do better.

- Be careful of the size of the penalty for misbehaviors. Although you want the gaining of a mistake point to be a small setback in your child's eyes, you don't want him to lose hope or the inspiration to do better.

- On the other hand, you may need to put a limit on the number of mistakes that can be made within one time period. Children shouldn't feel they can repeatedly slip just as long as eventually they end up with enough positive points.

- When you do have to give a negative mark, remember to tell your child that you're sorry she slipped but that you have confidence she will do better later.

- If your child becomes very upset when you fill in a negative mark, don't try and explain, yet again, why this behavior has to change. Sympathize by saying, "I know it's upsetting to make a mistake. But the thing is, you can make up for it another time." Then later, when your child is calmer, talk about what happened, why he slipped, and how he might avoid doing so next time.

For more creative and engaging ways of keeping track of negative as well as positive behaviors, look at the Pockets for Points chart and the Blue Lagoon chart in the Pull-Out section at the back of the book. (These charts are explained in more detail in Part 3.)

You've just seen how this plan can help to change behaviors. There's a reward in play. The process of working toward receiving it will necessitate learning new behaviors. The hope is that once the reward is achieved, these new improved behavior patterns will have taken root. But there are several less obvious benefits. I have referred to them earlier as the invisible rewards. They come with the territory and are the ones on which the permanency of these behavioral changes rest.

BEYOND CHANGING BEHAVIORS: THE INVISIBLE REWARDS OF THE REWARD PLAN

Although getting a child to brush her teeth thoroughly or shop without complaining or do her chores or be polite are all important achievements in and of themselves, there are some added perks to using a Reward Plan. Your child will naturally grow as a result of his successes, and the relationship between the two of you will involve trusting and pleasant interactions instead of angry ones. Everyone wins! Here's how:

- Your child's self-esteem will be enhanced. When parents pay attention to children's good behaviors rather than concentrating on the bad ones, children feel better about themselves. They see themselves as appreciated. They assume it's for good reason: They are great! The sense of accomplishment they experience as the line of stars lengthens, or the tickets mount up, or the check marks begin to overwhelm the chart, is palpable. Their self-image grows a bit with each added mark of recognition for a job well done.

- Children can exercise that need for independence. Remember the quest for independence? The Reward Plan is an opportunity for your child to choose. You're not making her do anything. She doesn't have to fight against your not-so-unreasonable demands just so she can feel like her own person. You're saying, "Look. I know you stand apart from me and you can make your own choices. You can have what you want, but here's the deal. You can take it or not. Your call." Of course, you are still the one ultimately in control, but once you have a Reward Plan in place, it is not your desires that are center stage. It is your child's, and she will feel it that way. Now, unfettered by your constant "do this" or "do that," she is left to make choices of her own.

- Your interactions with your child can become more enjoyable. When children become trapped in patterns of poor behavior, they often trap their parents into the same! Poor behavior often begets poor behavior. When's the last time your child, yet again, said something rude or ornery, and you smiled patiently, saying, "Oh, I can see you're not feeling very happy right now"? Quite likely, you snapped, criticized, threatened, or generally withdrew your affection. Your child then pulled away as well, brooding in the silence of his room. When next you met there was an uneasy truce, followed hopefully by some pleasant time, until the next time your child once again chose to display the exact behavior you cannot abide. And the cycle spins on and on and on. Wouldn't it be nice to put a stop to this?

- You allow your child to see the pleasures of working toward a goal. "Look at what I can do," the child will think proudly as she contemplates how good it feels to work toward something!

Nine-year-old Daniel always dragged his feet getting ready for school in the morning. He'd forget to put away the milk carton, leave his bed unmade, and lose his homework. Finally, his single father, Jacob, suggested that they make a list of required morning activities and keep track of them using a Daily Checklist (for a blank one, see the Pull-Out section). Daniel had been asking to rent a computer game on the weekends, and Jacob decided that if Daniel was able to complete the checklist at least four mornings each week before 7:30 a.m., he could earn the game. Daniel added one more detail: He wanted the chart to reflect who was ready first, he or his father! Over the following days Daniel learned to pace himself (he hadn't liked the last-minute rush either), felt proud of the way he could stick to it (he showed the chart to his friends), and enjoyed discussing which game he might rent with his dad—knowing it would be his if he persevered. Daniel learned it was kind of exciting to see a goal growing closer and closer and closer.

Hopefully, you now understand the basic principles behind a Reward Plan. You can see how it works and the many advantages it holds. But you might still have the nagging feeling that you are merely tiptoeing around (and sometimes sticking your toe into) bribery. You aren't. It's time to explore the differences.

Bribery or Reward?

A CRITICAL DISTINCTION

It is easy to suspect a Reward Plan of being a sophisticated way of bribing a child to behave correctly. In all fairness, the giving of rewards can approach bribery. A poorly played out plan (in which, for instance, a child receives a reward before the plan's closing date because she's acting up in a public place and her embarrassed parent offers the reward as a quick remedy) can indeed teach children little more than how to get goodies out of Mom or Dad. In other words, it is the *manner* in which you conduct the Reward Plan—the way you set it up and consistently stand behind it—that will determine whether you are actually offering a bribe or a reward.

It might be a good idea to pause here and consider what, really, is wrong with bribing. We all instinctively know it to be a dishonest act, but if we can dissect it a bit, the differences between a Reward Plan and bribery will, I believe, become clearer.

HOW BRIBERY GOT ITS BAD NAME

What does the *American Heritage Dictionary* say about the word *bribe*?

1. Bribery is anything, such as money, property, or a favor, offered or given to someone in a position of trust to induce him or her to act dishonestly.

2. Bribery is also something offered or serving to influence or persuade.

I suspect that the first definition springs to parents' minds and heavily influences their reactions to a plan that is based on behavior modification. They fear that they are being dishonest unless they teach children the inherent advantages of good behavior. In fact, they quite correctly assume they could be encouraging their children to take the cynical view that acting well is worth it only if "there's something in it for me." More specifically, parents are concerned that if they use rewards, their children might

- gain an inappropriate amount of power;
- demand gifts every time they are asked to do anything;
- feel no motivation to achieve or learn anything that takes effort without a reward;
- miss out on learning any benefits of good behavior along the way to earning a reward;
- lose the opportunity to experience feelings of pride over a job well done because they are motivated to achieve not the goal, but the reward;
- fail to develop strength of character that will allow them to deal with future difficult situations; and
- begin to see parents as gift givers instead of as people from whom they might gain wisdom and seek advice.

Are all of these fears reasonable? You bet. But a well carried out Reward Plan will help children understand and appreciate the reasons behind the behaviors you are seeking to encourage. Although your child may focus initially on the reward and on a newfound sense of control, as the days go by the new experiences of feeling successful and developing problem-solving skills will gain importance.

The fact is that rewards provide only a temporary incentive for children to try out new ways of behaving. The goal of a good plan is to instill in children the wish to use desired behaviors. But this wish can develop only when children experience the pleasures of doing the right thing—pleasures they hadn't known could exist for them. In inspiring this desire, a good Reward Plan moves away from the dark alleys of bribery into the sunlit fields of unanticipated benefits.

There are many ways to avoid the negative aspects of bribery when using a Reward Plan:

- Never introduce a Reward Plan immediately after a child misbehaves. If rewards are offered to children just after they engage in undesirable behavior, they may learn only that bad behavior ultimately gets rewarded.
- Once you've designed and agreed on a Reward Plan, in most cases you

must stick to it. The moment you allow your child to significantly lessen the requirements, or change the reward to something bigger, or speed up the timetable, you may be crossing the fine line between rewards and bribery. If you change a plan because you've given in to pressure from your child for an easier deal, he may learn that he can get what he wants by wearing you down. (Of course, it is always a parent's prerogative to revise a plan based on judgment and experience. If you see that you've set goals that are unrealistically challenging and you anticipate that your child may lose hope of succeeding, then a modification in the plan is quite justifiable.)

- Don't give in to outlandish demands. Stand firm about appropriate awards. They should be small but attractive—the idea being that the child is going to have to reach down into herself to find some motivation of her own. The reward is simply the necessary added impetus. If you promise the Taj Mahal (or PlayStation II), your child will not have the time or inclination to get in touch with her own desire to do the right thing.

REWARDS: ALL THAT THEY CAN BE

One key to rewards staying just that and not morphing into bribes is to offer the reward when a child's ability and desire to take command of his behavior for his own benefit are most available to him. Here are a few tips to help make sure your timing and approach are right:

- Wait for a calm moment. Don't offer a reward while the hysteria is in full flower. Introduce a thoughtful problem-solving approach when your frustration is at a low ebb and your child is in a mood to "hear" you and understand the plan.

Ten-year-old Emily had barely spent 5 minutes daily practicing her flute lessons during the past week. And despite her mother Bridget's nagging, minimal practice effort had become the norm of late. On Friday, Bridget decided that it was time to let Emily know that she needed to take practicing seriously if Bridget was to continue to pay for lessons. Although her mother knew that Emily was talented musically and prided herself on her flute skills, her social life was crowding out practice time. Bridget decided to discuss the problem on Saturday morning.

However, when Emily arrived home the next morning from a sleepover, it was clear she was tired and in a cranky mood. Her mother decided to wait for another time.

On Sunday, after Emily had had a good night's sleep, Bridget said, "I've been thinking about how it's been going with your flute practicing. I've been nagging you a lot but that hasn't seemed to make it easier for you to find time to practice. I'm wondering whether you still want to continue with flute lessons."

The tears that welled up in Emily's eyes gave Bridget the answer. "Well, I'd be happy to continue providing you with lessons, but I think we have to figure out a way for you to make more time for flute practice. Why don't we just organize a plan together so that I don't have to keep bugging you, and you can get the 20 or 30 minutes of daily practicing done that your teacher expects."

"I guess so," Emily said tentatively. She seemed uncertain of her mother's intentions and also worried whether she could live up to the plan.

Bridget continued. "I know you've been wanting a new dress for the flute recital. I'd be happy to buy you that new dress if you get into a groove with your practicing." Bridget then drew Emily into setting up a Keeping Track chart (for a blank one, see the Pull-Out section at the back of the book) that would indicate the number of evenings Emily did sufficient practicing. They agreed that if Emily practiced diligently for 21 days in the next month, she could get a new dress for the upcoming recital. Emily, inspired by the idea of keeping track of her progress and excited by the knowledge she would get the dress she yearned for, agreed to the plan smoothly. Her willingness to cooperate was due partly to her being able to listen to Bridget's reasoning. Emily entered the conversation in a fairly relaxed mood, and she was in an emotional space that allowed her to see the benefits of getting her practicing done.

- Encourage your child to come up with ideas that would help him make changes in his own behavior. Get him thinking about his habits, what he likes, and what he feels is a reasonable expectation. Your child will be involving himself in a plan that makes him captain of his own ship, and this will bring him great pleasure. (Remember the quest for independence!) The reward will of course remain bright, but it will be only a piece of the process during which your child will experience pride, satisfaction, and success.

- Treat the behavior you are trying to change as part of a whole experience. Point out that picking up toys makes it so much easier to find what she wants. If you are rewarding kind behavior between siblings, point out what a good time they would be able to have with each other (even if it's just in short spurts). Bribery focuses only on changing the current behavior and offers no benefits for life in general. The Reward Plan leaves room for approaching the problem from a richer perspective: What can you and your child learn along the way? What invisible rewards are lying in wait? How will it feel for your child to watch herself through discipline and perseverance successfully achieve a goal?

- Allow your child to participate in selecting a reward, but hold the line against outlandish requests. Remind your child, "This is to help get you going!" in a good-humored way. The implication? You expect your child to take over on his own, but you understand he might need a treat to start moving. A bribe is the be-all and end-all, whereas the reward is just a cog in the wheel.

BRIBES AND REWARDS: A CLOSE COMPARISON

I hope you are clearer now on what makes a bribe different from a reward. Still, it might be useful to look at some specific comparisons to further clarify the distinction. Consider the following situations and the different ways they can be handled:

Six-year-old Jessica whines and complains every time her mom takes her to visit Grandpa at the nursing home. She says she's bored. She ignores her grandfather. She treats them both to a litany of "When can I go home?" and "I'm so bored." By the end of the visit, her mom is worn out and embarrassed. She is desperate to quiet Jessica's complaints and to protect her father from his granddaughter's behavior.

- **Bribe:** Jessica's mother bends down and whispers that if Jessica will be quiet for the rest of the visit, they will stop and buy her a big ice cream on the way home. This idea sounds great to Jessica, and she's learned something, too: Behave poorly enough, and someone will "pay" you to stop. What an incentive to whine even louder next time!
- **Reward:** Jessica's mother grits her teeth and ignores Jessica's whining as best she can. She apologizes to her father. During a calm moment the next day, Jessica's mom sits her down and tells her that she knows it's difficult to visit a nursing home. It can look drab, feel sad, and smell funny. She encourages Jessica to describe how she feels. She listens sympathetically and allows for the possibility of shorter visits. Then she explains that Grandpa needs the cheering up, and she knows he feels happy seeing his granddaughter. Jessica's mom next states, in a *positive* tone, that she knows Jessica is able to behave far better than she does at the nursing home. She then suggests a way to make the task a little more pleasant for Jessica. She tells Jessica that if she can occupy herself during the visit (perhaps by drawing), do something nice for Grandpa, and avoid complaining, she will take her for an ice cream cone after the visit. She stays *realistic* by saying that they will stay only 30 minutes and that she will let Jessica know, quietly, when each 10-minute increment is up. True to her word, after the next visit, Jessica's mother takes her to an ice cream shop, where they both indulge in ice cream cones with sprinkles. Jessica is proud that Grandpa said, "Jessica, you were so much fun today!"

The reward in this story is connected to the mature behavior, and not to the whining and complaining. And, of course, there is the added benefit of unexpected praise. Jessica felt great that her grandfather expressed his pleasure in her. The next week, Jessica was yet again very pleasant and did nothing but engage her grandfather in conversation. She wanted a cone afterwards, but her mother got the feeling it had not been foremost on her mind during the visit.

Daryl, age 8, and his 6-year-old brother Trevor have a wonderful time in the playroom every day, but come evening, they drag their heels endlessly when asked to clean it up. The job is easy enough: Place the cars and trucks into the cupboard and the building blocks in a plastic bin, sort the crayons and pencils into their separate boxes, and toss all action figures into the toy box. Their mother has very long days at work, and all she wants is an orderly house in the evenings and two boys who listen.

- **Bribe:** Their mother walks in Monday evening and says, "Clean this up now." Fifteen minutes later she returns, and the boys are still playing. She repeats her request. "In a minute!" The boys' words ring like shrill bells through the room. Their mother snaps. "OK, if you clean up right now, you get two extra cookies for dessert." The boys immediately stop what they're doing and, grinning from ear to ear, practically run each other over neatening the room. It's a perfect job. It takes almost exactly a minute and a half.

- **Reward:** Their mother walks in Monday evening with an egg timer in hand. "Guys, please clean up," she says. As usual, she receives a fleeting acknowledgment of her presence. She doesn't get upset. Instead, she says, "Here's a timer. I'm going to set it for 5 minutes." She knows this is a *realistic* amount of time. "If you get this room cleaned up before it rings, you can have an extra cookie for dessert." She smiles. "It's up to you." Then she goes into the other room, kicks off her shoes, closes her eyes, and relaxes. At 4 minutes, she calls to the boys, "One more minute!" This positive reminder keeps the boys on track and recognizes they do not yet have a good sense of time. The bell goes off, and she re-enters the playroom. The room is as neat as a pin, and both boys are smiling smugly at each other.

Ten-year-old José dislikes reading. He's in day camp for the summer, and his dad wants him to read every evening. José balks. He reads 5 minutes and claims it has been an hour. He "loses" the book he's reading. They're fighting every evening.

- **Bribe:** José's father promises to buy him a bike as soon as he reads 10 books. So José looks for the shortest books he can find, "reads" them quickly, frequently skipping pages, and 2 weeks later demands his bike. His father can't really disprove that he's read the books, and so he feels bound to honor his commitment—regardless of the fact that José may not have honored his.

- **Reward:** Jose's father wants to give him an incentive to read over the summer. To ensure that he does in fact get the work done, he rewards José for the time he spends reading rather than the number of books. That way, the quality of what he does gets the attention, keeping the process positive. His father monitors his reading periods to be sure he stays focused. Whenever possible, he sits down with José and reads his own books. They decide together on *realistic* 20-minute reading sessions and agree that every time José finishes 10 reading sessions, he earns a trip for himself and a friend to the bowling alley. He loves bowling, and so José starts to read. Suddenly, he discovers that the second book he's chosen is actually exciting. Two nights he actually reads for 45 minutes.

José's father is modeling enjoyment of reading and teaching José the joy of it as well. José has "allowed" his father to do this because he's got an incentive. However, as time passes, the invisible reward takes center stage. José enjoys the bowling, but he learns he rather likes reaching for a book in the evenings as well!

REWARDS: UNDERCOVER MATERIALISM?

You may still question the wisdom of offering any kind of material reward. If we encourage children to work to earn rewards, be they ice cream cones, allowances, or toys of one sort or another, are we encouraging our children to become materialistic? And might offering "things" in return for behaving well in itself be bribery?

If they are selected carefully, I do not think rewards either encourage materialistic values or are tantamount to bribery. There are many ways to avoid the pitfall of materialism:

- Choose rewards that are not materialistic in nature. Young children can earn the opportunity to bake a cake with you or a trip to their favorite playground.
- Remember to consider yourself a reward! Special time with a parent, for any child, is usually a boon. They pick the game or activity, and you bring your whole self to the event.
- Save the larger rewards for problems that require your child to work very hard or to put up with something that is very uncomfortable. Working to stop the habit of thumb sucking, giving up play time to go for needed tutoring, or persisting in wearing a leg brace despite teasing from peers are examples of problems that might warrant a generous reward.
- You can attach rewards to something your child might get anyway but doesn't see on the immediate horizon. This has the advantage of being an impetus but not one that overshadows the lesson at hand.

Seven-year-old Jenny kept wandering out of her room at night a half hour after she was put to bed. The first time she did it, she complained of feeling scared, and so her parents allowed her to sit with them and talk for a little while before bringing her back to bed. Now Jenny expects this response every night. Before this, Jenny had been a child who conked off quickly. Her mom and dad selected the Daily Checklist chart (for a blank one, see the Pull-Out section) and told Jenny she would receive a star for each night she stayed in her own room and went to sleep. After 10 nights of this, they agreed she could get a new, larger set of markers. They'd actually been discussing this purchase with Jenny for a few days anyway, because the colors of her old set were fading. Drawing was her favorite hobby. Jenny was pleased there was a target date for the new set, and so she put some serious effort into staying in bed. Things got off to a difficult start (Jenny was very tearful and anxious at first), so her parents added into the plan that after tucking her in, they would sit in her room for 5 minutes while Jenny closed her eyes. This worked very well, and after 2 weeks had passed Jenny got her new set of markers.

Young children will rarely balk at having to earn things they ordinarily would have received for no change in behavior at all. They have no clear belief system about what they are "owed," so they often accept the new requirements without protest. To older children, however, you may need to explain that they now have to earn certain privileges so that you can begin to help them improve their habits. If you think your child might feel some resentment over having to work for something he previously received without effort, you could offer a small bonus. Pointing out the possibility of greater gain can ease resentment.

Ten-year-old Aaron had been receiving a $3 allowance for a year. The allowance had been set up with no strings attached. Aaron's parents expected him to do some chores, but he typically "forgot" to do them and rarely got to them without considerable nagging from his parents.

Finally, his father sat down with him, explained that he felt Aaron was old enough to assume more "mature" responsibility for his chores, and pointed out that his own paycheck was tied to work. He explained that he wanted to help Aaron prepare for the future, when Aaron would have a job. They filled out a Contract (for a blank one, see the Pull-Out section) together listing the several chores for which Aaron was responsible and the allowance he would receive if he completed all of his chores. His father decided that it would be appropriate to add $1 to

Aaron's allowance, as he was now going to be expected to carry out all of his chores in a more responsible manner. He told Aaron that he would get one reminder, but no more than that.

Aaron was happy about the increase and felt that the change in expectations had been recognized. He also felt proud that his father thought him old enough to start teaching him about the "ways of men." The respectful position his father had taken made it possible for Aaron not only to cooperate but also to learn what it feels like to really earn a dollar.

WHEN THE REWARD ISN'T WORKING: IS STEPPING IT UP A BRIBE?

I have been told many times that a reward hasn't worked, so the parents felt forced to up the ante. A movie turned into three movies. An ice cream cone turned into a sundae extravaganza. An afternoon roller-blading in the park became a party at Roller Blade City.

Is this bribing?

Not exactly, but it is getting awful close to bribery terrain. On occasion, parents may misjudge the appropriate size of a reward, and then increasing the attractiveness of the reward might be called for. But most times, if you've chosen an attractive reward to begin with, upping the reward is not the answer. Lack of success with a Reward Plan may mean that something else is going on with your child that the plan isn't addressing. In the next chapter, I will deal with the reasons your plan may not be working.

Suffice it to say that bigger and bigger rewards are usually a sign that there are hidden problems underfoot. Trying to cover this fact up with more elaborate rewards can bring you to the brink of bribery, mostly because your child is once again asking to be bought. Tragically, she may not even realize that she's really confused or upset inside about other things and is merely assuming that if she could just get something bigger and brighter, she'd feel OK about changing her behavior. Try not to buy into this. You'll be short-changing everyone.

Allow me to sum up the rather significant

differences between bribes and rewards:

- Bribes put an immediate end to only one event of poor behavior. Rewards end poor behaviors less quickly, but they establish a pattern of good behavior along the way.
- Bribes teach children that all they have to do is act badly, and all good things will come. Rewards teach children that they have to behave well, consistently, for all good things.
- Bribes offer no chance for a child to find motivation from within. Rewards require that a child reach inside himself for strength and fortitude.
- Bribes teach children nothing at all and stand no chance of ever doing so. Rewards can potentially teach children about the pleasure and pride of working toward a goal and about the many unexpected rewards that can appear along the way.
- Bribes encourage children to view their parents as people to manipulate. Rewards encourage children to view parents as fair, straightforward, clear, and trustworthy.

A FINAL NOTE: CONTRACTS— AN ANTIBRIBERY DEVICE

A Contract that spells out the rules and is signed by both parent and child can provide a way of underlining that the Reward Plan calls for mutual responsibility. Although Contracts can be useful simply for record-keeping purposes (as seen with Aaron and his father in the previous story), they also give an aura of seriousness to the plan. The message is that you both have a "job" to do. It has a beginning, a middle, and an end. If either of you fails to do what is required, the deal is off. The very concept of a Contract in many ways underlines the nonbribery aspect of the Reward Plan. Let's face it—bribes are sneaky things. Who signs on to a bribe in the light of day? The act of putting the terms down on paper makes it abundantly clear that this is a plan of which to be proud. There are no secrets. Your child isn't getting away with anything or manipulating anyone. The control rests with all participants.

Of course, the other advantage of having the Contract is that it minimizes arguments. Your child can't say, "But you said... !!" Or, rather, she can, but you only have to pull out the Contract and nicely say (avoiding the "I told you so" attitude you may be tempted to express), "Oh, but see. Let's read this together." She may grow rather sullen for a short time and could even choose to go on strike. At this point you might want to remind her (if it exists in your Contract) of any time constraints built into the terms. (For example, in exactly 2 weeks she has to have improved a particular behavior 10 times.) Also, remind her of the reward. You might even discuss it a bit with her. "Tell me again which movie you want to rent? What have you heard about it?" or "Just think about that ice cream sundae just waiting for you! Caramel or fudge on top? What do you think?"

Later in this book I will offer sample Contracts to use in other situations.

OK. It's time to design the Reward Plan you need for your particular child!

CHAPTER THREE

Designing and Carrying Out Your Plan

The Reward Plan approach is extremely versatile and usually quite effective for any child from age 3 and up. Beyond about age 10, children's increasing sophistication and determination to be in control of their own lives will make this approach less useful. However, there are certainly preadolescents who are young enough at heart to respond to Reward Plans, so you should use your judgment as to whether this approach would work with your 11- or 12-year-old child. The following examples will give you an idea of the many different kinds of behaviors this plan can improve:

- saying please and thank you
- picking up clothes or toys
- brushing teeth
- dressing quickly
- using tissues
- sharing
- letting others go first
- controlling temper tantrums
- decreasing fighting between siblings
- increasing kindness between siblings
- stopping thumb sucking or nail biting
- reducing whining
- letting others speak on the phone without interruption

- going to bed on time
- doing chores
- finishing *all* homework.

A Reward Plan can address any one of these issues, plus many more. The principles remain the same, no matter what behavior you are seeking to change. Nearly every detail of your plan, however, will depend very much on the nature of your particular child (age and temperament) and his or her problem (unfortunate habit or destructive behavior).

You should aim for a plan that works in the most *expedient* way. What do I mean by expedient? A plan that your child will respond to quickly and enjoy and that will leave everyone feeling successful and proud! This will usually require that the plan you choose take *context* into account. This chapter will help guide you as you assess your own situation and then go ahead to develop a successful Reward Plan.

SIZING UP CONTEXT: FACTORS THAT WILL AFFECT YOUR REWARD PLAN

You've probably discovered that many of the family routines and rituals that work in the homes of your neighbors and friends cannot be readily transplanted into yours. Your family most surely includes a unique blend of individual styles and has its own personal tempo. Before you do a thing, go through a mental checklist—what's unique about my child, and what's going on within my child at home, at school, and with friends? And what's going on in our family at this moment that might have an impact on my child?

★ YOUR CHILD'S TEMPERAMENT ★

There are some children who, as a matter of course, light up when presented with a new idea. "Cool," they think. "Something different." They're open. They're game. They're generally positive in their approach to life.

Then there are those children who resist change like the plague. It wouldn't matter if their T-shirts are nearly in shreds, their friends are starting to annoy them, or they're invited to an amusement park they've never seen. They'll want to keep the shirt, would refuse to meet new kids, and would want to see *loads* of pictures before reluctantly allowing themselves to be driven to Fantasyland.

And of course there are all the kids in between. Some are temperamental. One minute they're placid as can be, the next it feels as if you're sharing a room with a tsunami. Others find it hard to get enthusiastic about anything and tend to greet any new plan with a yawn.

When it comes to creating a Reward Plan for your child, it is important to recognize the sort of child you have and what will most likely grab his attention and keep him interested. Recognizing your child for who he is will influence the way you present the plan, how much you involve him in planning, the amount of time he will be able to wait before receiving a reward, and more. An enthusiastic child will likely want to help create charts, pick stars, hang the chart in a prominent place, and generally tell everyone about the plan. A more withdrawn child might simply watch as you create a chart and matter-of-factly place a check mark in the right spot as each day passes. (This wouldn't mean, however, that she isn't secretly enjoying her progress.) And for a child who hates change, you might need to go heavy on the shaping technique so that you aren't trying to alter too much too soon.

★ YOUR FAMILY'S TEMPERATURE ★

Although it is absolutely true that sometimes children misbehave because it is easier than being good, or because they want to feel independent, or simply because of poor impulse control, other times it can be an expression of their distress with you! Perhaps you have been too preoccupied with your own problems. It's possible you've been focusing on your children only when they act badly, as opposed to remembering to praise them when they do something well. They may feel abandoned and unappreciated if positive attention has been scarce.

It's also possible that your children may sense tension in your family. Although you may think your marital arguments are remaining behind closed doors, it's a rare child who doesn't pick up on unhappiness between his parents. Or if one of your children is troubled or exceptionally difficult, it may be very hard for the other child to feel safe and protected. Your "easy" child's behavior is bound to reflect her fears and anxieties.

It is very important that you consider how the family's emotional climate may be affecting your child before plunging ahead with a plan to change your child's problem behaviors. The Reward Plan cannot work if your child is struggling to "do good" in an atmosphere laden with unrest. He will need praise. Attention. He will need to feel as if he is bringing you pleasure as well as moving closer to his own. This cannot happen if everyone around him is showing frustration.

Now let's take a look at the process of actually developing your Reward Plan.

FIVE STEPS TO A SUCCESSFUL REWARD PLAN

OK, now, down to the basics. You've assessed your family situation and decided that there are no readily apparent obstacles to introducing a Reward Plan. If you follow these next steps and give a bit of thought as to how to customize the plan to your child and family, success should be right around the corner!

★ STEP 1: DECIDE WHAT THE PROBLEM BEHAVIOR IS ★

Although your child may have many troublesome behaviors, it is best to pick only one or two at a time to work on changing. Otherwise you may discourage your child from even trying. Remember, the Reward Plan has to feel realistic.

It's helpful to pick a behavior that your child knows has been troublesome. She will likely be a bit tired of arguing with you about it, and although she may not admit it, she may welcome a chance to stop the friction.

Be Specific

In identifying the behaviors you want to change, be sure to outline them specifically. It probably won't work to say "a neat room." What do you mean by that? Toys in the bins? Bed made? Clothes in the hamper? Do you also require a neat closet? The trick is to be *very* clear, so that halfway through the plan you're not arguing about the terms of the agreement. You don't want to hear your child cry out, "Hey! You never said I had to clean up my desk drawer!"

Specificity has another advantage. You can give a star for each piece of the deal, so that your child can see progress quickly. And yet one more advantage to breaking a goal down into smaller units is that children can receive partial credit on a day when they fail to perform the entire task. This will help give the Reward Plan a positive tone. "Gee, you can't get a star for picking up your clothes, but I'm glad you can get one for making your bed!" If the goal is 20 stars, he's still moving forward.

It's a way of underlining how much you are on your child's side.

Start Off Easy

Be careful to pick behaviors for which your child can earn rewards fairly easily. Brushing teeth every evening is simpler than performing a list of five self-care tasks. Hanging a coat on a hook every afternoon is far easier than cleaning up the whole playroom. If you go easy, your child can have a taste of what it feels like to strike a deal, work toward a goal, and succeed! Once she sees it is doable and a reliable way to overcome a hurdle or meet the demands of a task, she'll be less reluctant to stretch herself.

Also, be sure the period of working toward the goal is not too long for your child. Younger children will find it harder to hang in for long before getting a prize. Some young ones may need to receive a small reward right away. Others will be able to wait until the end of the day, and perhaps even as long as a week. The ability to delay gratification is undeniably one that grows with age.

Obviously, if rewards need to be given frequently, they must be small ones. If you are going to ask your young child to wait briefly, you must clearly present the connection between each good behavior and the reward. For example, if you plan to offer your 3-year-old a small plastic dinosaur after he has urinated in the toilet four times, you might draw four Xs on a Design-Your-Own chart beside a drawing of the dinosaur. Then explain to your son that each time he goes to the toilet by himself, he can cover an X with a star. After he covers four stars, he gets the dinosaur. (For an illustration of this chart in use, see p. 33.)

Older children can wait longer. An 8- or 9-year-old child can work for 1, 2, or 3 weeks—in most cases, at maximum a month—to earn an attractive reward. Just be sure to find a way to track her progress using a chart, a notebook, or the kitchen calendar, and your older child will be assured by the growing line of check marks that her efforts will eventually pay off.

★ STEP 2: SELECT A CHART AND A REWARD ★

The previous chapters have mentioned a number of charts, awards, and end-of-plan rewards. Let's take a look at how you should go about selecting a particular chart and reward for your child. More in-depth understanding of how charts and rewards work together will be provided in the scenarios in Part 2 (Sample Reward Plans).

Choosing a Chart

Often, the chart you choose will be the one that most conveniently tallies points toward a reward. However, the chart format itself can sometimes be rewarding, particularly with younger children. A number of ready-to-use imaginative charts with scenes that you or your child can apply stickers to can be found in the Pull-Out section at the back of the book. (Each one is described in more detail in Part 3.) These are called *My-Own-Picture Charts* and are ideal for 3-, 4-, and 5-year-olds. For example, the Welcome to the Zoo chart depicts a zoo scene with empty cages. This can make the reward of animal stickers much more exciting than they would be without one's very

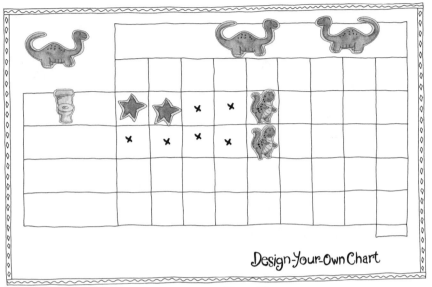

Design-Your-Own Chart

Choosing a Reward

Often you will be able to decide on an appropriate reward yourself. You know your child's wants, and you know what size reward would be appropriate. However, in some cases you may want your child to participate in designing the Reward Plan.

When you decide to involve your child, it's not a good idea to begin a planning session with no real idea of what you think would be appropriate. First of all, your child could catch you off guard by requesting something tantamount to her own private screening room, and then you might be so thrown that nothing small but tantalizing will come to mind.

Another major mistake is agreeing to a reward in a moment of desperation. Aside from smacking of bribery, this could later cause you regret. Remember, a key to the Reward Plan is that it is a plan. It's not a "knee-jerk, I-gotta-get-this-kid-to-stop-acting-like-this-right-now" solution.

So walk in with what I call a *reward profile* in mind. How big? Will it be something you do with your child or give to your child? Will it be something he's been asking for, or should it be something new he's never thought of? Come prepared with a few options. And let your child's age level guide your selections.

Younger children (ages 3 to 5) are usually pleased with almost any present or surprise and are often content with stars or stickers placed on a colorful chart or affixed to their shirt or jacket. Although children ages 5 to 8 will also enjoy the simple process of receiving points, stars, or tickets, their plans will work best if they have a more significant incentive. An outing, a special activity, or a small toy at the end of the plan will usually do the trick. Older children, ages 8 and up, will tend to have more expensive tastes and defined likes and dislikes. They will lose interest in the format of the chart if the ultimate reward doesn't shine brightly enough. Again, this is not to say you have to hand over your Swiss bank account, but walking in

own zoo. The opportunity for your son to become zookeeper and to continually build up his animal collection may thus be reward enough to entice him to change a problem behavior.

In other cases, novel charts or alternative awards, which are grouped in Part 3 as the categories *Tracking With an Imaginative Twist* and *All the Extras,* can provide at least part of the excitement and appeal of a Reward Plan, so that the final reward can be kept quite modest. For example, the Treasure Hunt chart adds the fun of hunting for the reward. Prize Coupons, which children can hold and color (as Sally did in the Party Departure Plan in chapter 1), also add more allure to the prize for which they can be traded. You may want to spend some time browsing through Part 3 when looking for a chart or award item that would particularly appeal to your child.

An imaginative chart format certainly will not always be sufficient to motivate children to work hard at changing behaviors. Particularly with older children, and many times with the youngest ones as well, you will need to add an end-of-plan reward to provide adequate motivation. Older children will view gimmicky charts as kid stuff, so the Keeping Track chart or Daily Checklist, which merely provide a simple format for record-keeping, will usually be your best choice. All of these charts (and more) appear at the back of the book so you can tear them out and start with a few items or activities in mind that are modest but still strongly desired will be very helpful in motivating your older child.

If your child attempts to engage you in endless discussion about rewards, you should be prepared to do what a professional negotiator would do: Calmly announce that if your child doesn't decide on one of three or four acceptable rewards within a specified time, you will not be able to begin the plan. No matter how much you yourself want to start working on getting rid of the problematic behavior, stick to your word. It's a rare child who won't quickly decide she'd better take the offer that's on the table!

★ STEP 3: INTRODUCE THE REWARD PLAN TO YOUR CHILD ★

Younger children usually easily accept a Reward Plan. Handled well, it can be like a game for them. But older children may be a bit more skeptical. They realize first and foremost that they are being asked to improve a behavior (or get rid of one). The reward certainly sounds good, but they may still have doubts about whether they want to change the behavior. It's smart to explain to them in a straightforward way what you have in mind.

"Jamal, I've been thinking a lot about how we keep getting into arguments about your homework not getting done." This surprises 10-year-old Jamal. Perhaps for the first time, it sounds as if his mom Sylvia is more concerned about the fighting than the work.

"I really don't like these arguments any more than you do, so I've been doing some thinking about a plan for helping you get things done that would work better for both of us. I know that Mrs. Evans gives homework with a lot of writing, and I know that writing is hard for you. I realize that when you think through problems in your head, you think really fast and well. But Mrs. Evans's grades are based a lot on the homework you hand in, and I don't think you've been very happy with the grades you've been getting on your homework." (Here, Sylvia is identifying an underlying difficulty for Jamal, which he will be glad she understands. She is offering empathy for the struggles he experiences and his own likely disappointment in his grades . . . never mind hers!)

"Because you have to work pretty hard on your homework, I've been thinking it would be reasonable to offer you a reward if you put a little more time and effort into it. I know myself that when I have something to look forward to, I'm able to push myself a little harder." Here Sylvia is presenting the plan in a way that sounds informal and mature. After all, it is a way she herself approaches problems.

"I thought that if we could try to figure out a way that you could sit down earlier and get your homework done, you could earn a reward at the end of each week. You've been asking to rent video games, and perhaps you could earn a video game rental if you complete your homework by 8 p.m. every evening for a week. We could make a weekly calendar and check off every day that you manage to do this. If you do have a late soccer game, we can make an exception for that day."

"That's cool about the rentals," Jamal says just a little warily. "I mean, thanks for thinking of this, but that 8 p.m. thing is bad. My favorite show is on at 7:30."

Sylvia counters. "Can you think of another way to get your homework done so you can earn the video game rental?"

"I could do half of my homework before the show—I could do the hardest part with the most writing. Then I could finish it after the show," Jamal proposes.

"That sounds fine, as long as you don't end up being too tired when the show is over," Sylvia replies. "How about we try it for a week and see whether your homework grades improve?"

In this last part of the conversation, Sylvia has provided one of the most critical ingredients in a Reward Plan: She's allowed her child to have his say in the actual plan. She allowed him to negotiate. This, especially for an older child or any child who has trouble giving up control, is a very important component of putting together a plan. The key, however, is not to let the negotiation get out of hand or go on at great length with equal passion. You're not at the Camp David peace talks.

One nice healthy go around, and I'd say that should do it. Maybe twice, if you sense that if you just give a centimeter more, your child will acquiesce with good will.

As much as possible, you want to eliminate the idea that you're in control. The point is that you both are. A Reward Plan requires that each person do his part. This is a very inspiring message for a child. Daddy isn't *making* him read every night for 30 minutes. Mommy isn't *forcing* him to put his shoes in the shoe bag in his closet. What your child has here is an opportunity. It's a chance to willingly engage in a plan to improve his behavior and to assure himself a reward for the effort.

One way to make your child's involvement, responsibility, and control obvious to her is to ask her to participate in the planning and creation of whatever chart you use. If she's the artistic type, she may want to decorate the chart with all kinds of drawings or simply add some color to the black-and-white charts. This activity might interest her more than even the discussion of how many days she has to remember to set the table before she can get a reward! An older child might be more interested in working out the time frame. But you might still suggest that she put a personal touch to whatever chart you create. It's a way of making the plan *hers.*

And, of course, allow your child, if he wants, to post his own stars or check marks or reach for his own tokens. He's rewarding himself that way. The same goes for any other part of your plan that could invite your child's regulation of his own behavior. If you decide to use a kitchen timer to mark a specified amount of time during which your child is to sit and read, he can set it himself. Then let him be the one to proudly announce, "Time's up!" As I mentioned earlier in the book, children relish being the captain of their own ship. But there's another bonus, too. By letting your child enjoy his own success and reward himself with a star or self-congratulatory announcement, you're saying, "Go ahead. Be proud of a job well done." You want your child to feel good about himself—self-approval is a great thing.

In fact, it's the most important kind of approval.

★ STEP 4: FOLLOW THROUGH! ★

You may be very tired one day, your child particularly crabby, and the events of the day a bit too much to tolerate. Try and keep to the plan anyway. If your child refuses to get into bed at the agreed on hour, sympathize with her loss of a star but hold firm. If she won't brush her teeth, then regretfully she won't be able to earn the token until tomorrow. Your child will keep moving forward if she sees you mean business. This is true especially at the onset of the plan. If she discovers that the rules can be bent on a cloudy afternoon, she may take advantage.

Try not to unilaterally stop a plan midway, either out of your own fatigue or your child's lost interest. Instead, illustrate the importance of the goal by making a point to find a relaxed time to sit down and discuss it. Perhaps you're asking too much, or the settled on reward no longer holds any luster, or your child is feeling overwhelmed by other problems. Talk it through, letting your child know the goal is still one you would like him to achieve but certainly in a way that works for him. "Gee, Brett, I'm having trouble again talking on the phone. Are you still into getting that action figure?"

Or you might comment, "You started off earning stars like gangbusters. Suddenly you've stopped! Is anything filling up your mind and pushing thoughts about this plan out? I know your Dad hasn't called for a few days. Are you missing him?" Because children usually have a hard time identifying what's bothering them, it can be helpful to offer your best guess.

Then, make it clear *you're* not giving up. "Well, look, I think we still need to work on a plan for you to stop interrupting. You know that making phone calls from home is part of my job, and that's how I earn money. Let's see if we can make this plan work."

Whatever you do, don't fight about the plan! The last thing you want to do is end up chiding your child for failing to earn points. This is supposed to be a positive experience. If you find yourself about to say, "What's the matter with you? Don't you care about the reward?" bite your tongue.

Just talk it out as best you can. If necessary, find another place to vent your parenting frustrations!

★ STEP 5: ENDING THE PLAN ★

Recognition. That's almost all it takes. "You did it!" and "I'm proud of you!" are perfect remarks. They underline that your child did what she set out to do and succeeded. You might also want to offer her an "I Did It!" Certificate (see the Pull-Out section at the back of the book).

The other thing you have to be careful to do is to deliver the reward *promptly*. Your child has waited long enough. If you want to change other behaviors with this technique, you really must deliver. Within reason there should be no fuss, no excuses, and no delays.

To keep boredom at bay, any future plans may best be done using different charts or a different token system. This is one reason why Part 3 contains a large variety of charts and award items. And do keep in mind that if your child has earned a particular privilege, you will likely have to keep it up after the plan is over, provided his behavior stays in line. If he's earned the right to an extra half hour of watching television on his favorite night, you can't exactly take it away from him now that the plan has been successfully completed!

BEHAVIOR CHANGE: TEMPORARY OR PERMANENT?

With the exception of simple habits that become automatic, it is generally important that some form of incentive be present so that your child can maintain motivation.

But I am referring here to those invisible rewards, such as

- ongoing praise for your child as she continues to treat her little sister well;
- your child's own realization that in fact a B+ feels a lot better than a C-; and
- pleasant times at the dinner table, including joke telling, rather than arguments about using knives and forks.

As I mentioned earlier, sometimes children need an incentive to get over the hump of relinquishing poor behavior and to see what positive things come from simply behaving well. Usually, after a short while, the pluses are so obvious that many problematic behaviors will stop. Your nail-biting daughter finally gets to see what a little pink nail polish can look like on her newly grown nails. Your children who, before rewards, could not share now see how nice it is to have double the toys to play with. Your cavity-prone son can finally, having learned to brush his teeth regularly, enjoy a trauma-free visit to the dentist.

Behaviors can become permanent simply because they bring rewards of their own.

But what if they don't? What if your child goes back to nail biting, squabbling with siblings, or a dry toothbrush? Bad habits don't disappear easily, and you may have to go for round 2 with a new plan. Over time, with gentle encouragement and structure from you, plus incentives to sweeten the way, Reward Plans together with consistent, supportive parenting will solve a good many childhood problems.

TROUBLESHOOTING PROBLEMS: WHEN THE PLAN JUST DOESN'T WORK

Sometimes the Reward Plan simply does not work. It could be the wrong time. Your child may need another kind of intervention. You may need to be in another mood. The reward may be too small. The behavior may be too ingrained to change quickly. Your child may yet have too limited an attention span. The atmosphere in the house might be too tense for anyone to want to please anyone else. You might need to wait a while to let some key factors shift a bit before trying again.

But in the meantime, the following are areas for you to troubleshoot when the plan does not seem to be taking hold. This list isn't entirely new; I've touched on these issues throughout these first three chapters. It is not necessarily a toolbox for fixing things, but I'm hoping it will be helpful for you to examine these factors one by one just to see where you stand. If you are able to figure out what might be going wrong, chances are the next Reward Plan will work.

★ THE REWARD SIMPLY ISN'T ATTRACTIVE ENOUGH ★

This is the most obvious problem, but it's amazing how easy it is to miscalculate! A young child might at first be gleeful over stars and then, midway through, lose interest, not realizing there's another option. He could get a reward too! Our children often mature in ways we're not aware of, and so we make assumptions that are no longer correct.

Mary watched as her 5-year-old daughter Tia placed her first star on the chart. She'd actually cleaned up her art table at the end of the day.

"Pretty!" Tia said with a satisfied smile. Mary felt great, too. The second evening, Tia proudly put another star on the chart. A different colored one. "Look!" she exclaimed.

"Beautiful. You are doing so well!!" Mary smiled.

The third night Tia forgot the star. Just like that. Mary reminded her about cleaning up, and Tia easily enough stood up, put her crayons away, and then stuck a star up next to the other two. She nodded with

satisfaction. "Great!" Mary said.

The fourth night Tia didn't want to clean up.

"But Tia!" her mother exclaimed. "Look at the row of pretty stars!"

Tia looked at them for a long moment.

"Stars are OK . . ." she said softly. "I'll put stuff away 'morrow."

Tia likes stars. But she's a little old for them to hold much allure. Her mother might have done better with a series of stars ending with a new art supply box.

★ YOUR CHILD IS JUST TOO YOUNG, PERIOD ★

Think about what this plan requires: Delayed gratification. Stick-to-itiveness. The ability to understand the passage of time. Patience. Motivation from within. The ability to recognize invisible rewards along the way. Self-control.

Goodness! That's a tall order! Just because next week your 2-year-old will celebrate her third birthday does not mean she's magically leaving behind the negativism of the 2s and is now ready to collaborate with you. If your child is clearly frustrated, unable to tell you she hasn't earned enough stars, or can't seem to grasp how come she doesn't have the cupcake with the candy face yet, chances are she just doesn't get it! You are simply introducing a game that isn't right for her developmental stage. So skip a turn and give it a spin later.

★ THE BEHAVIOR IS TOO TOUGH, RIGHT NOW, TO CHANGE ★

Maybe you are expecting too much. If you've just brought home a new baby and your 5-year-old is no longer picking up his toys, this may not be the time to attempt to correct his behavior with a Reward Plan. For one thing, it's normal for your child to be jealous and cranky and to want to act like a younger child. You can't change his feelings. Also, in trying to change his behavior, you will be missing what he really needs—time with you! In other words, sometimes a difficult behavior is born of feelings that have to be attended to before the behavior can disappear. Were you to try to get rid of the behavior without dealing with the feelings, chances are a different unwanted behavior would erupt. Again, this is where a strictly behavioral approach doesn't work. Sometimes, you have to address the whole child within his world—not just his outward behavior.

★Other Family Members Are Not With the Plan★

It's possible that you have the strength to stick with the plan, but your mate is just too tired and, when left alone with your daughter, is unable to enforce the rules. With this situation, it's a toss-up as to whether the plan will work. Your child may find a way to demand a star when she doesn't deserve it, or she may simply become so confused by the on-again, off-again nature of the plan that she stops trying. If this happens, you may need to back up a step and work toward agreement among all adults in the house.

★You Are Attempting to Eliminate Behaviors That Other Family Members Exhibit★

Katherine was 5 days into the plan to stop 8-year-old Tim from using foul language. He'd been doing beautifully. Another 5 days, and he was getting three packs of baseball cards.

Katherine and her husband Bill had just sat down to the dinner table with their son when Bill accidentally spilled a glass of water. He had had a bad day with his boss and snapped, "Sh_t!" loud enough for the People's Republic of China to hear.

"No fair!" Tim announced. He turned and stared at Katherine in an accusatorial fashion. "If he can, I can!"

"I had a bad day," Bill tried to explain. He said it with exhaustion and without any conviction. He seemed, Katherine noted, to have completely forgotten the chart.

"I didn't like school today either," Tim replied. "It was a sh_tty day!"
Katherine sighed.

The best you can do when a parent or other role model exhibits a behavior you are seeking to wipe out is to explain that the adult, in your opinion, is making a mistake. Certainly you can underline that this adult is a terrific person but that everyone could stand to improve. Katherine might say, "Dad should not have used that language. But he had a miserable day, and it just fell out. Years ago, he learned a bad habit, and we don't want you to learn the same one. Bad habits are hard to change, and the earlier you start to change them, the easier the job will be." And if Bill might be willing to participate in efforts to change *his* behavior, he could have his own chart and reward!

★Your Child Has Gotten Attached to Negative Attention★

There are many reasons for a child to behave poorly and then somehow feel satisfied by your negative response. She may not be getting enough attention for her good deeds and thus is happy to bask in any interaction with you. If it takes a misstep, well then, she'll give it to you. She might also be reacting to tension in the family. If there are problems between you and your mate or between you and a sibling, she may be unconsciously trying to take some of the pressure off that interaction. It might feel better to draw away some of the negativism toward herself than to sit back and watch helplessly while others tangle in unending arguments. Her good behaviors, she may unconsciously conclude, will only inspire everyone to look away from her and back to the unrest brewing elsewhere.

★YOUR CHILD CANNOT TOLERATE ANYTHING THAT SMACKS OF CONTROL★

Some children are extraordinarily resistant to anything that makes them feel as if they are being controlled. In truth, it's difficult to escape the "if-you-do-this-then-I'll-do-that" aspect of the plan. The best thing to do with a child like this is to first allow the Reward Plan idea to just go away. This will be saying to your child, "OK. Guess what? You are in control. We don't have to do it." Then after a little time passes, you might want to bring this idea up again but *not call it anything*. As soon as it has a name, your child will see it as something designed by you. Instead, play to his ability to independently make a decision that will end up with a fun result.

"Brian, I know you've got a really good memory, and I'm puzzled how you can keep missing so many spelling words all the time. You must really hate studying them. But you don't seem very happy with your grades. Look, it's up to you. Get at least an 85% on three of the next four quizzes, and you can earn something—maybe your choice of desserts for a week in your lunch box? It's up to you. Let me know what you decide."

The more independent your child feels, the more likely he will be to follow along.

SUMMING UP

The thing about the Reward Plan is that you learn the most about what works and what doesn't by putting it into action. Everything I have presented to you so far is theoretical and instructive. You have to make it your own. You have to do it, feel it, see what works and what doesn't, and learn from the experience.

There is no one exact right way to carry out this plan, which is as it should be. I stated at the beginning of this book that the problem I have with behavioral techniques is that they often ignore the wonderful idiosyncratic nature of human beings and the ways in which they interact with their environments. Your child is unique. Therefore, the way in which the Reward Plan will work for you and your child will be slightly different from the way it works for others.

Which brings us to perhaps the biggest, most important invisible reward: The Reward Plan requires that you actually *know* your child—what's on her mind, what turns her on or off, and how to best motivate her. It also requires that you know yourself—your limits, your parenting style, your preconceived notions about where your child *should* be, as opposed to *is*. Finally, it engages the two of you in a goal-oriented plan that is filled with good will. You have to connect. You have to acknowledge. There is a built in shared pleasure.

In many ways, the Reward Plan will change more than just unwanted behaviors. It can alter in the most positive ways how you and your child relate, creating an atmosphere of increased trust and understanding.

Actually, what a splendid reward for both of you.

Time for Action: Sample Reward Plans

Introduction

So far, you've gotten some sense from the short vignettes of how Reward Plans work. Now I want to provide you with a more detailed understanding of how to develop your own plan and put it into action.

The sample Reward Plans in Part 2 are organized into chapters that treat seven of the most common challenges parents must help their children face:

- getting along with others
- keeping to the schedule
- overcoming sleep problems
- establishing hassle-free hygiene
- getting along with siblings
- doing the chores
- reducing homework blues.

In each chapter you'll read a detailed description of a problem behavior that will probably be familiar to you in some way (for example, an anxious child who cannot fall asleep alone). Next, you will see how the child's parent puts together a Reward Plan that fits the child's age and personality. You'll read how the parent first talks about the problem with the child. (What kinds of scary thoughts bother her when she is alone in her room?) Then you'll see how the parent describes the details of the plan (the parent will sit on a chair that moves further and further away from the child's room) and explains the chart and reward chosen to use (the Treasure Hunt chart—together with a variety of small "treasures" as the reward). Finally, you will see how the action plays itself out and learn about the invisible rewards that parent and child come to enjoy (suddenly, the child is enjoying feeling like a big girl and able to comfort herself).

Then two shorter descriptions of Reward Plans for other problems follow, so that each chapter covers the most typical areas of concern in each problem category. Finally, I also include a brief list of additional challenges for which a similar plan might work. So if you don't find the exact behavior you are seeking to improve in one of the vignettes, be sure to check out those lists!

Which brings me to a very important point.

The plans here might work exactly as described, but it is highly probable that you will have to incorporate your own ideas to adapt these plans to the needs of your particular child.

The sample Reward Plans in this book feature children that are a range of ages, temperaments, and family backgrounds. The plans are meant to provide a kind of buffet from which you can choose appetizers (ways to talk with your child), entrées (plan details), and desserts (reward ideas) that will satisfy your specific needs. Select the ideas that you believe will help your *particular child* benefit from these plans, which are really, at their core, motivational tools.

For example, your 5-year-old son may have the problem of 5-year-old Heather in chapter 6, who won't sleep through the night without your company. But he may not share Heather's temperament, so you will need to modify the steps in the Reward Plan. Or your 8-year-old daughter may resist bedtime like 10-year-old Eric, but her resistance may not be related to the arrival of a new stepfather in the home. So you will need to adapt your approach to address the reason for her resistance.

Just as children differ in personality and in the way they respond to parents' rules, adults themselves differ in the kinds of behaviors they are willing to tolerate in their children. Daily hair washing may be a high priority for some parents, whereas others may feel that perfectly clean hair is not worth that much of their parental energy. Because putting together a

Reward Plan involves effort on your part, you'll want to save your energy for the behaviors you find most troubling.

Sometimes similar difficult behaviors are shared by two or more siblings, and at times entire families face common challenges. In the sample Reward Plans, I've provided examples as to how you can set up a plan to get two siblings working cooperatively together. Chapter 5 shows how a carefully thought out plan helps both Rebecca and Steven stop their morning procrastination behavior, and chapter 8 describes a Reward Plan that helps two brothers get along better by offering incentives for kind behaviors and penalties for hurtful interactions. And in chapter 9, Mom and Dad themselves participate in a family plan aimed at getting chores done in a more efficient and pleasant manner.

The sample Reward Plans in chapters 4 through 10 use a variety of charts to monitor progress. To some extent, the choice of chart is up to you. If you're closely following a sample Reward Plan, you may want to use the chart featured in the plan so that you can feel confident about how to put the plan into action. Or you may decide to choose a different chart that's more appropriate to your child's age group or that you think will be more engaging for your child. Keep in mind, however, that if your plan involves a penalty for misbehavior, you will need to choose a chart that allows you to keep track of negative check marks or points. More guidance on chart selection is provided in Part 3, and ready-to-use charts to get you started can be found in the Pull-Out section at the back of the book.

The Reward Plan approach also allows you to choose from a wide variety of sizes and kinds of rewards. Whenever possible, a modest reward is best. You will see that 4-year-old Alex is able to stop grabbing toys with the minimal reward of dinosaur stickers that he can arrange on the Dinosaur Land chart. However, 7-year-old Kendra needs the incentive of a new bike to motivate her to cooperate in giving up playtime with her friends and working hard at tutoring lessons to overcome her reading disability.

Do keep in mind that these are *model* plans! Don't be discouraged if your first attempt at a Reward Plan is not as successful as the ones described here. In fact, you'll likely have to work out some bugs as you explore the best way to put a Reward Plan into action. If your first attempt at a Reward Plan fails, you might want to read through a few more sample plan chapters for further ideas. For example, if you are developing a Reward Plan for your 5-year-old daughter, you may want to read several plans for children close to her age. Or if your son is particularly anxious or impulsive, you may do well to review the plans involving children with a similar temperament. And remember to look back at the Troubleshooting Problems section in chapter 3 if you continue to have difficulty setting up a successful plan.

With some work on your part, and perhaps with a little tinkering along the way, your Reward Plan should provide benefits that far outweigh the effort you commit to putting a plan together. It's a great feeling for you *and* your child to find ways to get out of ruts in which you've been stuck. Overcoming a behavior problem once and for all, or simply achieving a few weeks or months of improved behavior, can boost everyone's self-esteem and demonstrate that when one works at a problem, change is possible!

And if improvements don't last forever, you may need a refresher. Just choose another chart or move to a different reward. That's the beauty of the Reward Plan approach.

Listen to your child. If he says, "Well, can we do it this way?" give it some thought. It might work beautifully. It's also a way of saying to your child, "I want to help you do well *your* way."

What a respectful approach to teaching your child!

This book is about you and your child working together toward a goal you both understand and are motivated to achieve. Both of you should own the plan and immensely enjoy the results together.

So, pick the situation that is creating the most serious problem for your child, look for the plan that most closely targets it in this book, and get started.

Everything that follows is bribe free and *very* rewarding!

"You're Not My Friend Anymore!"

GETTING ALONG WITH OTHERS

We are all social beings. We all want and need to reach out—to be understood, to be appreciated, to be loved. From the moment your child was born, she sought connection with you, responding to your touch, then following you with her eyes, then smiling . . .

Remember the pleasure you both experienced the first time you could play peekaboo or clap hands together? You were connecting. You were showing your child how much you care and encouraging him to be there in the moment with you. It came so naturally, and it was so exciting.

But of course as your child grew, so did her social awareness. It wasn't just you and her. There were other people out there with whom she had to relate. And before she knew it, she was in the land of social norms. Now she is expected to follow certain rules. To think not just of herself. To interact with some modicum of respect for others.

As your child's unique personality begins to express itself in more and more obvious ways, the conflict between social norms and a natural, "unsocialized" personality becomes more of an issue. With many children, grabbing, shrieking, complaining, and demanding are now on the menu. Taking toys without asking, pushing peers when they get in the way, and demanding that others "do it my way" are often standard fare. Or perhaps your child, so bubbly and full of sunshine when alone with you, turns pale and heads for the shadows when strangers appear. Reward Plans can help even when social problems are age-appropriate.

If you are like many parents, you probably reacted with dismay to the emergence of socially unappealing behaviors. You might even have thought, "What's wrong with my child? Why can't she be nice? Who is ever going to like her? How is she ever going to have friends?" But then you figured out ways you could teach her. Step by step, you could show your child how to relate to others.

Although social skills do seem to come more easily to some children than others, they are not something that comes naturally. Young children are simply too egocentric to think about what others need or feel and too inexperienced to realize that if they don't start doing so, there will be no play dates in the offing. Certainly, recent research indicates that the capacity for empathy can start in the toddler years . . . but that doesn't mean the willingness to put aside one's own needs does!

Maybe you have a shy child who has trouble reaching out, or one who foists himself on others to the point of being rude, or one whose inborn inflexibility makes it hard for him to moderate his own behaviors. Perhaps he is very aggressive and when displeased hits first, or he's so sensitive that the smallest tease sends him into tears.

Such ways are hard to change.

This is why the Reward Plan can be so effective. Certainly it's a good idea to make a regular habit of speaking to your child about how she feels in social situations and about how she thinks others feel. You will want to encourage her to put herself in others' shoes. And of course you will want to talk with your child if you think her feelings have been hurt by others and help her figure out how best to protect herself.

But along with these routine activities, there may be times when you need to motivate your child to do the right thing. A child who is temperamentally impulsive, demanding, or aggressive just may want to be the boss or keep the best toys for himself, and that's that. He will need a little help "letting go." At the opposite end of the spectrum, the temperamentally withdrawn child who lets his own inner anxiety rule his behaviors might be able to move outward only if he is encouraged to do so by a tantalizing reward. Of course, what neither child will realize, until he's experienced the results, is that happy social interaction is a reward in and of itself.

Just watch a 4-year-old who willingly shared a toy suddenly find herself hugged by her little buddy. Pure joy.

Although a young child may not immediately realize the connection between considerate social behaviors and being liked by peers, you can begin to help him realize that one thing leads to the other. The reward encourages him to try out new behaviors. Then you have an opportunity to reflect with him on the good result.

Most children in the end will be so pleased with the social outcomes that they will want to continue even when rewards stop. A Reward Plan will give them that extra push they need to discover the pleasures that come to you when you treat others with respect and appreciation.

NO GRABBING TOYS!

Four-year-old Alex loves his play dates. His peers, on the other hand, don't always appreciate him. When Alex covets one of his friend's toys, he simply grabs it. "Let me play!" he says with urgency and then pays little heed to the ensuing protests.

In fact, he acts like the taking of another child's toys is his birthright. Alex doesn't seem to understand why his friends get upset and angry or hit him. He's thinking about how much fun it will be to play with this toy. Alex doesn't give a thought to how his friends may feel.

His mom, Melanie, has tried coaching Alex to use words when he sees a toy he likes. And she's often suggested the 5-minute rule, allowing the children to play with a toy for 5 minutes and then to trade. Before every play date, she reminds Alex that he has to share and that he can't simply grab a toy away from a friend. He has to ask first. "Can I play with that now?" Melanie suggests he ask and, if put off, to respond with, "OK, but can we trade in 5 minutes so I can try it?"

"'K," Alex says amicably, but 30 minutes into the play date, Melanie usually hears cries from the other room. She then finds Alex sitting with a look that vacillates between confusion and annoyance, clutching a toy he has clearly yanked from the other child's hands.

The truth is, Melanie has had it. She's also noted that very few parents call to set up play dates. She has to make the calls, and more often than not, she hears hesitation in the other parent's voice.

She's worried that Alex is grabbing his way into social exile.

★ FIRST, TALKING ABOUT IT ★

Right before the next play date, Melanie sits down with Alex and says that she knows he is very happy that he's going to spend the afternoon with his friend. She tells him that she knows it's a lot of fun to play with other kids and that she thinks it's great when he does.

Because Alex always enjoys stories, Melanie decides to make up a story starring Alex that will provide some guidance in a playful way for improving his social interactions. After she's prepared a simple story, she reads it to him:

Alex is a handsome boy who likes to play with his friends. His friends bring their toys when they come to his house. Alex wants to play with his friend's dinosaur. He asks, "Can I have a turn?" His friend says, "No, it's mine." So Alex says, "Can I have a turn after 5 minutes?" His friend says yes. Alex runs and tells Mom that he can play with the dinosaur in 5 minutes. When Alex's turn comes, he brings one of his dinosaurs to his friend and says, "It's time to trade." Alex and his friend now can have fun playing with different creatures!

Alex smiles and says, "Hey, that's like me!" Melanie grins and says, "I have an idea how your play dates can be more fun. My plan will help you to remember to take turns."

Alex is thrilled. "What is it?"

"*Dinosaur Land!*" Melanie sings out.

★ THE REWARD PLAN ★

Melanie pulls out a sheet of dinosaur stickers and puts them on the table.

She explains that during the play date, when he wants a toy, he has to *ask* for it and not just take it. "But what if he doesn't give it to me?" Alex asks. "Remember what Alex did in the story? You will ask if you can have it in 5 minutes and come tell me to time it," Melanie replies.

Alex is comfortable with that and reaches for the sticker sheet.

Dinosaur Land Chart

Alex is wild about all sorts of animals, but particularly dinosaurs. Melanie shows Alex the Dinosaur Land chart (for a ready-to-use one, see the Pull-Out section at the back of the book) and explains to Alex that he can earn a dinosaur sticker to place on the chart each time he remembers to ask to play with a toy and waits until his friend gives it to him. Alex eyes the *Tyrannosaurus rex* sticker. "This one first!"

"Perfect!" Melanie answers approvingly. "You know, Alex," she adds. "I think we should practice first so that you can think about what to say to your friend. You be you, and I'll be Tommy, and let's pretend I have a toy you want." Melanie picks up a brontosaurus. "Can you ask me nicely to play with it?"

Alex asks nicely, and Melanie applauds.

"OK, now, I'm still Tommy," Melanie says. *"No, it's my dinosaur."*

Alex looks confused, and so Melanie reminds him that he must say, "OK, but can I play with it in 5 minutes?" Alex slowly repeats the words after Melanie.

Again, as Tommy, Melanie pauses, and then replies, "OK, if I can play with yours." Alex giggles at his mom's impersonation of Tommy.

"But whatever happens," Melanie says, "What don't you do?"

Alex grins. "Take it."

"Right," she agrees. "Use words."

★ WHAT HAPPENS ★

To ensure the success of the plan, Melanie decides to tidy up and pay bills near enough to the playroom so that she can see and hear what's going on. Early on she notices Alex beginning to reach for a toy in his friend's hand, and so she quickly and quietly calls out, "Remember the sticker!" Alex drops his hand and asks his friend if he can play with the toy. He then runs over to Melanie and asks to put the Tyrannosaurus rex sticker on the chart. She gives it to him, along with a hug, and then suggests that he quickly select the next sticker he will earn.

Alex does so, runs back to his play date, and in 5 minutes is back again having asked to play with another toy. Melanie laughs to herself; she is not at all sure he really wanted to play with Tommy's stegosaurus because he has the same one himself, but she lets him take another sticker. She is glad that he is practicing the new social skills.

As it turns out, during the first afternoon play date, Alex earns 10 stickers. He forgets and grabs a toy only once. At that point, Melanie steps in to remind him and quietly adds, "Sorry, no sticker this time, but I know you'll earn another one soon." Alex nods agreeably.

When Tommy leaves, Melanie compliments Alex on how beautifully and generously he played with his friend today. She asks him if he noticed that Tommy got upset only once! They didn't fight much at all. Alex grins happily. "Felt good, didn't it?" she asks.

He nods. "No yelling," he adds solemnly.

Melanie reads the "Alex story" again before the next two play dates, and again they use the chart. To hold Alex's interest, Melanie has purchased a new set of dinosaur stickers. Toward the end of the second play date, Alex starts to forget to request stickers, although he continues to ask appropriately to play with toys. After the friend leaves, Melanie offers Alex five stickers, the approximate number of times he used words to request a toy. He affixes the stickers with a smile, and Melanie hangs the chart in the playroom as a gentle reminder. She also awards him a Gold Medal (for a blank one, see the Pull-Out section) on which she writes, "First Prize for Great Sharing!" Alex is very pleased when Melanie offers him a yellow marker to decorate it, then glues it to a piece of cardboard and attaches a gold ribbon so he can wear it around his neck.

Alex's social behavior has improved considerably. He still occasionally forgets and grabs a toy, but when Melanie steps in to help Alex and his playmate negotiate, he agrees to use the right words.

A couple of weeks later a new friend, Brett, comes over. It turns out that Brett has not yet learned the skills that Alex has recently acquired. After Brett grabs one of his toys, Alex comes running into the kitchen to tell you. "Maybe he needs a sticker!" Alex whispers.

★ THE INVISIBLE REWARDS ★

Melanie can tell that Alex has truly learned some new skills. He clearly feels happier during his playtimes. And gradually, she notices that more parents are calling to set up play dates.

Melanie is so pleased with Alex's success. And she's

proud that she was the one who was able to help him.

★ ALSO WORKS FOR . . . ★

A Reward Plan using a chart and fun stickers works well for young children who are excited by simple rewards. The opportunity to create their own sticker picture enhances the attractiveness of the stickers. A sticker chart plan encourages desired behaviors without offering a penalty for unwanted behaviors, although you might add a time-out consequence if some sort of penalty is needed. The rewards are clearly linked to the desired behavior because the child receives one the moment he acts appropriately.

You might use this kind of program to encourage such behaviors as
- saying please and thank you instead of "give me" and silence,
- using words instead of hitting or throwing toys, and
- clicking the door closed instead of slamming it.

USING WORDS INSTEAD OF FISTS

Rachel and Joshua's 7-year-old son Matthew is a high-spirited boy. That's the positive perspective. Unfortunately, he is very physical in his interactions with other kids, and some children view his pushing as aggressive. He is a bit overweight and, as is typical during the elementary school years, cruelty has entered the picture. A few boys in the neighborhood have started to call him "Blimp Boy."

Rachel and her husband are worried that Matthew is feeling more and more hurt by the teasing and because of it is striking out increasingly often. His tendency to be physical with peers is indeed turning into aggressiveness. This is going to make things worse, for sure. In her most frightened moments, Rachel fears that her son will end up utterly friendless.

★ FIRST, TALKING ABOUT IT ★

After yet another unpleasant play date, Rachel finds Matthew sitting in his room looking very forlorn. "Am I fat?" he asks her. She smiles at him sympathetically and says, "No, you are not fat. You are a little heavier than some of your friends. At your age, kids will pick on anything that's different about someone." She adds that it's mean for anyone to say he's fat, but children often try and hurt people by telling them things they *know* will sting. The more sensitive he allows them to see he is, the more they will likely tease.

Rachel does, however, tell him that hitting and pushing aren't going to help anything. In fact, it can make things worse, because aggressive behaviors like that make people want to fight back. She suggests that what might help is to try throwing a compliment to his friends. It's hard to tease someone who has just said something nice about you. But he does need some new ways to respond to the insults if they do come. She tells him that sometimes it can be helpful just to ignore insults. Other times, it works to speak up for yourself and say you don't like it.

★ THE REWARD PLAN ★

Recognizing that it's hard to be the one to make a change, Rachel introduces Matthew to the Keeping Track chart (for a blank one, see the Pull-Out section at the back of the book). She tells Matthew that if he works hard at not hitting other children when they come to his house for play dates, his father will take him and a friend to an amusement park. Rachel chooses this reward because she hopes the trip will strengthen his relationship with a friend, keep their minds on the exciting rides, and also be an active outing involving his father. Joshua has been expressing concern that Matthew spends so much time indoors and gets little exercise. Rachel is also worried about Matthew's weight and the fact that his angry behavior has made it hard for him to join other children who are playing ball games on the street.

Rachel designs the Reward Plan to include play dates at their home only, so that she and Joshua can monitor Matthew's behavior. She knows that even if they miss one of Matthew's combative behaviors, his friends will come running to tell them. She explains to Matthew that he can earn check marks in the first column of the chart (which she labels "I Did It!") if he does not hit when others tease him. He can earn an additional check mark in the same column if he instead either changes the subject or says, "I don't like it when you say things like that. Stop it." (An illustration of Matthew's chart can be found on p. 123 in Part 3.)

As a bonus, to keep the tone of the program positive and to encourage Matthew to learn some behaviors that will make him more popular, Rachel also offers to give him a check mark if he compliments a friend. (Again, she will place the check mark in the "I Did It!" column.) She discusses with Matthew some positive things he might say to friends. Matthew decides he could compliment one friend on his skill with a popular video game and another for his talent at skateboarding.

Matthew will receive check marks in the second column of the chart (which Rachel labels "I Goofed") if he hits or pushes. In the third column of the chart, she will record the day of the play date. When Matthew has had five play dates with one or no "goofs" and earns at least 10 check marks in the "I Did It!" column, Rachel tells Matthew he'll be off to the amusement park with Dad and a chum!

★ WHAT HAPPENS ★

Matthew eagerly calls a friend to come over, volunteering, "I got a new video game. It's fun, and I bet you'll be good at it." Rachel enthusiastically gives Matthew his first check mark (for a compliment) in the "I Did It!" column. When the friend arrives, the boys head straight for the video game set and begin to play. Matthew offers another compliment and runs into the kitchen to tell Rachel, who observes that he's now ahead, 2 to 0!

After a half hour of playing inside, Rachel suggests the boys go out to shoot some baskets in the backyard. Because Joshua is working in the yard and can keep an ear out, this seems like a good opportunity for some outdoor playtime. Another friend shows up, and Rachel anticipates that Matthew may now get teased. He's not very good at basketball. She pulls Matthew aside, tells him he's been doing great, and reminds him of his goals. Then she lets Joshua know what's happening so that he can monitor Matthew's behavior. Before long Joshua overhears an insult. Matthew is quiet for a moment and then finally says, "I don't like those words!" Joshua notices that Matthew looks a bit forlorn for a moment, but then gathers himself and rejoins the game. No further taunts are sent his way, and he happily spends a good half hour running around.

Finally he comes into the house and heads straight for the chart.

"Bumper cars!" he murmurs to himself as he looks at the chart. Joshua follows him and adds another two check marks in the "I Did It!" column. "Good job, pal!" Joshua says as he thumps him on the back.

Matthew doesn't know it yet, but he is developing an excellent tool for keeping cruelty of others at bay.

Attitude.

In the meantime, the amusement park shines bright . . . which, at this stage in Matthew's life, is as it should be.

LEARNING TO GREET ADULTS

Tamara is 9 years old and painfully shy around unfamiliar adults. Actually, she is not much better with those she knows. She can neither look them in the eye nor say hello. She walks in and, if spoken to, lowers her head and mutters something approaching "uh-huh," then moves away as quickly as she can. It's startling. Almost seems rude.

Shawnelle, her mother, realizes that Tamara must be very uncomfortable, but she can't help but feel embarrassed. It's as if she has brought up a child with no manners. Many adults look at her on meeting Tamara as if to say, "What's wrong with her?" Shawnelle tries to sound calm as she states, "Tamara is very shy," but inside she is cringing.

Now a family reunion is drawing near, and Shawnelle wants to help Tamara try and overcome her anxiety—both for Tamara's sake and her own.

★ FIRST, TALKING ABOUT IT ★

The first thing Shawnelle works at is to understand her daughter's shyness more fully. A discussion with the school guidance counselor helps her understand that it's a trait Tamara was born with. She can't help it, and she is genuinely very uncomfortable in unfamiliar social situations. Shy people aren't shy every moment of the day, which is why Shawnelle has been confused by Tamara's lively behavior with her good friends. It's the unfamiliar that often gets to a shy person.

The counselor suggests some tools for Shawnelle to use in helping Tamara, including the following:

• rehearsing with Tamara some opening lines, such as "Hello, nice to meet you" or just a simple, friendly "hello." Shawnelle has Tamara wait in a room, then Shawnelle enters, sticks out her hand, and says, "Hi, Tamara!" She keeps at it until Tamara says in a strong voice, with her eyes on Shawnelle's, "Hello!" While engaging in this role play, Shawnelle avoids mentioning to Tamara that when she looks away or doesn't say hello, she appears rude; this observation would only add to Tamara's angst. Instead, Shawnelle emphasizes that smiling at someone and saying hello will give the person a chance to see what a nice person Tamara is.

- suggesting things Tamara can do to ease her discomfort in a room bustling with people she doesn't know. Shy people often feel that everyone is noticing how quiet they are or that they are disappearing into the woodwork. Either way, they feel frozen, uncomfortable, and lost. Shawnelle suggests that Tamara go study a painting on a wall, check out the food table, and if she's feeling OK, smile at someone. One great trick is to wear something unusual that she can talk about, like a necklace or funky belt buckle. Someone is sure to ask about it, and she'll have things to say.
- making sure Tamara knows that Shawnelle is her buddy. She can walk around with her mom provided that when Shawnelle introduces her to people, Tamara acknowledges them nicely.

★ THE REWARD PLAN ★

Shawnelle tells Tamara that if she can say hello to 10 people while looking them directly in the eye at the family reunion, she will reward her with the canoe outing she has been craving. To keep track of the number of times Tamara says hello appropriately, Shawnelle decides to wear slacks with pockets and to put a handful of pennies in one pocket. Each time she sees Tamara say a direct hello, she will transfer one penny to the other pocket. She will also put her hand on her daughter's shoulder as a signal that she has earned a point. The hand on the shoulder will have the additional benefit of providing emotional support to her shy daughter.

★ WHAT HAPPENS ★

At the reunion, Tamara has a little trouble at first because too many people come over at the same time, and she doesn't know where to look. But as other adults approach her with smiles and questions about her bright hand-printed scarf, she begins to relax, and the pennies start their journey from one pocket to the other. After one successful discussion, Shawnelle leans down and whispers, "Great job!" Shawnelle notices that when she is next introduced to someone, Tamara speaks louder and looks happier. Realizing the power of her emotional support, Shawnelle tries to say something supportive whenever she can do so inconspicuously.

A week later Shawnelle is in the canoe with Tamara, surrounded by a few other canoes holding complete strangers. "Hey, you're good at this," the mother of a young girl in the next canoe calls out to Tamara.

Tamara looks away shyly, and Shawnelle whispers, "How about 'thank you'?"

Tamara glances back at the woman and calls out, "Thanks. It's fun."

Shawnelle is thrilled. Tamara created her own lines.

Tamara holds her face to the sun proudly. She won her trip and actually spoke up on her own. It's an "outing" of sorts times two!

"Will You Please Hurry Up?"

KEEPING TO THE SCHEDULE

Children do not value the limitations of time. It's that simple. They want what they want, when they want it, for as long as they want it. They are oriented to the present. They don't like to be told it's time to leave, stop, start, or go if it doesn't suit their purposes at any particular moment.

There is, they tacitly assume, plenty of time for everything.

The more children are aware of consequences, however, the more interested they are in watching the clock. Older kids, aware that a school detention may be in the offing, may be eager to wear watches.

Unfortunately, most younger children don't recognize the more subtle but nevertheless unhappy consequences of getting off schedule. They don't equate their crankiness in the morning to hitting the pillow too late at night, and they cannot begin to appreciate that if they're late, you're late, and when that happens, your boss isn't pleased. In short, staying on schedule is something most children neither enjoy nor care about.

Add to this the many reasons children have for not wanting to get up in the morning (bed feels *so* cozy), or go to school (the person at the next desk has been teasing relentlessly), or make it home in time for dinner (the other kids on the block are still out), and things really become difficult.

To be perfectly honest, even for adults staying on schedule can be quite trying! And because schedules are prone to change (an after-school activity ends 30 minutes later, or summer breaks the momentum, or your boss needs you to stay an extra hour), a fair amount of flexibility on your part is required. Children don't usually see or appreciate your flexibility, and they certainly don't imitate it!

Unfortunately, when it comes to family life, if one person falls off schedule, it usually affects the others. So if you've got children who are resisting the demands of the clock, you've clearly got a problem you need to fix. And keep fixing. Although Reward Plans sometimes solve schedule problems once and for all, often you will need to periodically reintroduce a plan, perhaps each time with a slightly novel twist. This is because it's a major effort for children to mind the time and not their own rhythms. In fact, for some it's a Herculean task. But at least for a while, the right Reward Plan can do the trick.

This chapter provides an in-depth sample Reward Plan for
- two siblings ages 8 and 6 who dawdle in the morning, plus briefer plans for
- a 7-year-old girl who resists getting to tutoring lessons and
- a 10-year-old boy who is perpetually late for dinner.

OVERCOMING MORNING MADNESS

It's a few weeks into September, and 8-year-old Rebecca and 6-year-old Steven are still having trouble most mornings getting in gear. Each of the children has a different sticking point. Steven is a slow dresser, taking nearly 5 minutes for each sock because he is so easily transfixed by whatever toy his eyes happen to rest on. Gina, his mom, has tried encouraging him to get dressed in the bathroom, but he keeps wandering back to his room. Rebecca gets dressed without a problem, having laid her carefully chosen outfit out on the chair the night before. But it takes her so long to select a breakfast, and she eats so slowly, that Al, her father, thinks he could consume a five-course meal in the same amount of time. Gina tried just going ahead and preparing a yummy-looking breakfast one morning, but Rebecca would have none of it.

By the time the four leave, there isn't a dry eye in the house, and it isn't tears of happiness. Gina and Al have been late for work three times this month because of the children's dawdling. It has to stop.

★ First, Talking About It ★

The next Saturday morning, when there is no urgency to get out of the house, Gina sits down with Al and both children. "Your Dad and I haven't been enjoying our mornings very much," she begins, "and I don't think you guys are either. There's so much yelling."

Steven looks down at his feet, and Rebecca shrugs.

"I'm wondering if there's a reason you both are having such trouble getting ready for school? Steven, getting dressed seems like a big chore for you, and Rebecca, you seem to get really stuck on breakfast."

Steven looks a little sad. Gina suspects that part of his problem is the adjustment to first grade from kindergarten. The teacher has a lot more rules. "I think it might be very different in school this year," she says to him sympathetically. "Bet it's not so easy to have to follow lots of rules."

Steven nods. "Kindergarten was fun," he mumbles.

"First grade is hard at the beginning," Al agrees. "Probably it seemed more like play time last year. But you're a big boy now, and you'll be learning to read this year. And you'll be doing some fun projects, too. I really think you'll get used to it before too long." Then he turns to his daughter. "Rebecca?"

"I'm fine," she chirps. "I just like to . . . uh . . . think of stuff while I eat. You know, like my princess book and that doll with the new . . ."

"You're daydreaming," Gina says with a little impatience.

"Look," Al jumps in. "Mom and I end up doing a lot of nagging and yelling, and by the time we all leave the house I think no one is happy. That's not a great way to start the day! But we have some ideas about how we can all feel better about getting ready in the morning. And if it works, I think you'll both like the treat we have in mind."

★ THE REWARD PLAN ★

This plan has to take into account two children. Gina and Al have got double trouble!

Each of the children has strengths and weaknesses, and their parents want them both to succeed. In fact, for everyone to get out on time in the morning, Gina and Al *need* them both to succeed. They decide to use the Design-Your-Own chart (for a blank one, see the Pull-Out section at the back of the book) and to target three morning activities: getting dressed by 7:30 a.m., deciding what to eat within 5 minutes, and being out the door by 7:50. Gina and Al realize that each child will be particularly challenged by one of these tasks. They briefly consider whether they should include both children on the same chart or use a separate chart for each child. They decide to structure the plan so that the children must work together to get out the door on time, so they settle on a single chart.

Al asks the children if he can take a picture of them yawning so he can cut it out and paste it on the chart. They love that idea. Gina suggests they give stars for each goal achieved: red for Steven and blue for Rebecca. She explains that the children will need to earn a total of 30 stars each week, or 15 stars for each child.

As the reward for earning all their stars, Gina and Al will give them $2 apiece and take a trip together to the local dollar store. They tie the rewards together because they are hoping the children will motivate each other.

"But what if Steven doesn't get ready?" Rebecca insists. "Will I be able to go to the store anyway?"

Knowing her children, Gina anticipated this problem. If Rebecca earns all her stars one day but Steven doesn't, there will be several unpleasant consequences. Steven will likely have a tantrum, Rebecca will become angry at the thought that at the end of the week she will have to wait to go to the store, and one parent will still be stuck. If one child isn't ready to go, but the other is, either Gina or Al still can't leave the house!

So, Gina comes up with the idea of a Gold Star for cooperation as a way of keeping the children on track if one is having a bad morning. If one child is at risk of not earning a star, the other can earn a Gold Star by helping keep the other on track. The Gold Star will make up for a red or blue star lost by the other child. Thus, if they put in effort on their own part and add a little teamwork, they can easily make their weekly goal of a grand total of 30 stars.

Together they decide that if one child is behind schedule, the other child can ask, "Do you need help?" If the other child accepts help and gets back on track, the Gold Star will be awarded. So even if Steven isn't dressed by 7:30 a.m. on the dot, if he accepts Rebecca's help, the Gold Star they earn will ensure that they won't be lacking any stars. The children actually shake hands on the deal.

Al titles their Design-Your-Own chart "Beating the Morning Clock" and lists the three morning activities the children have decided to work on one below the other in the column of larger rectangular spaces at the left side of the chart. He adds one more item, "Help each other if necessary." Al then lists the 5 weekdays in the first 5 blocks above the grid of squares, and in the far-right-hand upper block he writes "Star Total" so he can add up the stars they win during the course of the week. As each child earns a star, Al or Gina places it in the appropriate space on the chart.

★ What Happens ★

The plan brings about significant improvements in the children's morning behaviors. Rebecca rises to the challenge and makes quick decisions about her breakfast menu. In fact, she mulls her breakfast choices over as she dresses, so by the time she arrives in the kitchen, she knows whether it's a morning for cereal, toast and eggs, or bagels and cream cheese. Steven also beats the clock. For the first 3 days, he's dressed pretty quickly.

However, on Thursday he fails to earn a star for getting dressed on time, and a tantrum is about to ensue when Rebecca swoops in with his shirt and pulls it over his head. Steven is at first annoyed, but then he smiles when he is made to understand that he and Rebecca have earned a Gold Star for cooperation, even though he missed his red star for getting dressed. Gina suggests to Rebecca that she come up with another way to help if this happens again, and so that evening Rebecca puts Steven's clothes out for him, the same way she does for herself. She glows with pride over her cleverness. Steven is back on track on Friday.

Saturday morning they're in the dollar store.

The plan works well for 3 weeks. Toward the end of the period, Rebecca and Steven begin to forget about the stars. They are also less excited about the trip to the dollar store, having purchased the items they were most interested in. But now they've settled into the routine, and Steven especially is less apprehensive about going to school.

The schedule runs smoothly until late winter, when both of the children are recovering from the flu. After having been out of school for almost 2 weeks, Steven is hesitant to return, and Rebecca is back to procrastinating over the breakfast menu. Al suggests they start a new plan using a similar chart but a different reward. Now, the reward will be breakfast at the pancake house on Saturday morning. The children's interest is rekindled, and the family is back to smooth mornings. At the restaurant, Rebecca is allowed to take as long as she likes deciding!

★ The Invisible Rewards ★

There's nothing worse than sending children off to school with angry feelings. You will feel guilty all day, and your children will probably walk into the classroom glum and annoyed. However, once your children are able to keep on schedule, you will all be more relaxed, and at least on some days you'll have a moment to say a warm good-bye and wish each other a nice day. As a parent, you can bask in that loving moment on and off all day. Your children will not be quite as aware of its value, but they will start the school day feeling good and in control. They will have been fueled by your approval and pleasure and will surely move through the day with increased confidence.

A chart that maps out a schedule so that the children can meet the bottom line is very effective. It breaks up the available time into pieces and minideadlines so that the children can keep track of where they are in terms of time to spare.

This approach is extremely good for helping children be punctual in getting to

- religious services;
- music lessons;
- therapist (speech, occupational, physical, psychologist) appointments; and
- sports practice.

GETTING TO APPOINTMENTS

Seven-year-old Kendra is a bright little girl with a reading disability. Nora, her mom, felt that the school's reading program was insufficient, and so she was very lucky to find her a place in the local university's reading clinic at the Graduate School of Education. At least *Nora* thinks they were lucky. The program is run by eager, well-supervised graduate students, is free, and is reputed to be of excellent quality.

But Kendra couldn't be more miserable. It's tough enough that her friends know she has trouble reading and has to attend a special class in school. This is something that embarrasses Kendra tremendously. But it turns out that Kendra's 4:45 p.m. appointment at the clinic on Tuesday afternoon conflicts with a regular social event: Kendra's friend's mother takes a group of girls to the roller skating rink. Kendra loves to go but always has to leave early to go to the reading clinic. If Nora could possibly switch the appointment she would, but Kendra has to attend the tutoring sessions when the time is available.

Fortunately, Kendra can squeeze in about 45 minutes of skating with her friends before she has to leave. Unfortunately, the moment she sees Nora arrive to pick her up, she starts racing around the rink. Nora practically has to yank her off the ice as she passes by, and once off she tears up. Her friends have given up asking where she's going, as Kendra repeatedly insists, eyes down, "No place. It doesn't matter."

By the time Nora has her in the car, she's usually crying, they're 10 minutes late, and it takes Kendra 20 minutes into the hour-long tutoring session to recover.

Many times Nora has asked herself if the extra help is worth this unhappiness. But the answer is always yes, and so she realizes that something has to be done.

★ First, Talking About It ★

Nora waits until late Saturday morning, when Kendra is usually relaxed and at her favorite spot in the house, her painting easel. "Kendra, honey," she begins, "I know how much you hate going to tutoring. I understand that it's scheduled at a really bad time, and it gets in the way of being with your friends at the rink. I'm sure you wish you didn't have to go at all and that reading could be easier for you."

Kendra puts down her brush, looking teary. "I'm a good artist. I'm just a little dumb." For a moment Nora is surprised. She hadn't realized Kendra thought her learning problem meant she was stupid. Nora thought this had been explained at school, and she can remember telling Kendra herself that she is a very bright girl.

Apparently, getting pulled out of classes and attending special tutoring sessions have spoken louder than words.

"Listen, Kendra," Nora says, taking her hand. "You're very smart. You just have trouble making sense out of letters on a page. This does not require smartness. It requires that a very small part of your brain work in a certain way. For you, things get a little mixed up in that part of your brain. But you know, lots of children with reading problems are extra good at other things, like you are at painting. The part of your brain that helps you to draw works extra well!"

Kendra looks a wee bit encouraged, so Nora continues. "You are getting help so that you'll be able to read well in spite of it!" Kendra shrugs. "Remember, your tutor gave us a book on reading disabilities for kids. Do you want to read that with me?" She never has before.

Kendra shakes her head irritably. "Maybe later."

"OK, look," Nora plows ahead. "I know it feels terrible to have to get all this extra help. You've been working very hard and giving up things to learn, and I'm proud of you. It's tough leaving the rink. But you know, it's really important that you work on your reading skills. So I have an idea about how to reward you for your efforts that I think will help you tolerate having to get to those lessons on time."

"Like what?" Kendra asks, as if her mother couldn't possibly come up with anything that would make up for her loss. She heaves a sigh. "What? An ice cream cone?"

★ The Reward Plan ★

Nora has thought long and hard about this, and she has decided that a significant reward would be appropriate. The stakes, after all, are high. She wants Kendra to get the extra help she needs early on, before she experiences too much failure. Also, if they continue to be late, Kendra may not be able to hang onto her appointment. There's a line of other families waiting to be accepted.

"No," Nora says, matter-of-factly ignoring her sarcasm. "I know you don't like the hand-me-down bike you've gotten from your brother. I was thinking that if you can get to tutoring on time, and without too much complaining, after 8 weeks you can get to pick out a new bike."

Kendra's eyes widen. This she hadn't expected. "Really? I could maybe get a bike like Monica's?"

"Absolutely," Nora responds. "Let's figure out exactly what you'll have to do."

Nora pulls out a Keeping Track chart (for a blank one, see the Pull-Out section) and lists the dates down the first column, leaving the next column for check marks indicating successful Tuesdays. Then she places a tape recorder on the table. The bike is a big reward. The terms have to be very clear. Because Kendra cannot read very well, they will record the agreement on tape. Kendra is a little surprised by this, but also amused. Nora includes Kendra in working out the terms of the contract.

Nora and Kendra agree on the following terms, which Kendra recites into the tape recorder:

I, Kendra Walsh, agree that I will leave right away when it is time to go to the reading tutor. I understand that I am smart and I have great ideas, but I have a problem learning to read. A tutor can help me so I will be able to read like my friends. I will try to get into the car calmly and to work hard at my lessons. If I manage to do this for 8 weeks, I can pick out my own bike as a reward! I understand that to keep it, I must continue to attend my tutoring sessions on time.

★ What Happens ★

Kendra's behavior changes immediately. She's a little bit mopier than Nora would like the next Tuesday, but she leaves the rink in a reasonable amount of time, and although she's not in the greatest mood as the tutoring begins, she picks up steam. The tutor says that all the kids are like that!

Eight weeks later, Kendra is ready to pick out a new bicycle. "I will get a reb dike," she writes proudly. Nora is thrilled; Kendra has never wanted to write spontaneously before. Then Kendra looks at her work and rewrites it: "I will get a red bike."

Kendra smiles proudly. She gives Nora a hug. Nora suspects she's thanking her for more than the bike. She smiles and hugs her daughter back. Understanding her child is truly a gift to both of them.

BEING ON TIME FOR DINNER

It's July, and Rick's 10-year-old son Michael is enjoying every minute of his summer days. After he arrives home from camp, he grabs a snack and heads right out to play with neighborhood friends. They play baseball, explore the woods, and visit the local pond to feed the ducks. It's actually quite delightful for him, but Rick does want him home, on time, for dinner at 6 p.m. Rick works evenings and cherishes the 45 minutes (all right, half an hour) he has to sit and talk with Michael and his wife together as a family. But despite the fact that Rick bought Michael a watch and told him when to come home, he finds himself calling Michael's friends' houses to track him down at dinnertime. Michael's friends' families clearly have a different routine, but Rick can't help that.

This is something Michael does not understand. Once home, he is sullen and unpleasant at the dinner table because his playtime had to be cut short.

As a result, the brief time Rick has with him is ruined.

Michael has wanted a dog, it seems, for forever. Rick and his wife have been seriously thinking about it and might have simply gotten their son the pet without strings attached. However, Rick decides to connect the gift of a pet with Michael's dinner behavior. The relationship between the two issues actually works nicely. Rick wants to emphasize that taking care of a pet involves responsibility and scheduling, and so does making it home on time for dinner. It occurs to him that Michael may not like leaving "the guys" early for dinner, but he might very well have to do that anyway to take his dog for a walk!

★ First, Talking About It ★

Over dinner one evening, Rick broaches the subject with Michael. He begins by saying that he realizes that Michael is unhappy having to leave his buddies to come home for dinner. He must feel as if he is missing out. Rick says this to make it clear that he understands the pull Michael experiences. Rick explains that despite this pull, it is very important for the family to have some time together and that Rick wants and needs him to respect that. Michael nods sullenly.

Then, Rick explains that he knows Michael would

like to have a dog, but that it is a very big responsibility. Michael has to stay on top of the time and understand that a dog is a living thing that needs attention. It may not always be convenient to take care of a dog, just as it isn't fun to come home on time for dinner. Michael insists that he can do what is necessary to take care of the dog.

★ THE REWARD PLAN ★

Rick agrees that Michael is probably up to the job, but he tells Michael that he needs to be sure, as Rick is too busy to contribute much to the dog's care. Rick and his wife sketch out the basics of a Reward Plan. It's simple. Michael must be on time for dinner for one month. If he does this, he can have a dog.

Michael thinks about the plan all evening and in the morning comes to Rick and asks, "What if I mess up once? Does that mean I won't get the dog? Sometimes I may forget to look at my watch." Rick compliments Michael about how carefully he has thought about the plan and agrees that, occasionally, he might not make it on time. Rick suggests that Michael can be allowed four late nights during the course of the month. The two decide that a good way to keep track is to put check marks on the kitchen calendar for every dinner he makes on time.

★ WHAT HAPPENS ★

Michael, Rick can tell, is psyched. As expected, he is on time for one week straight, eagerly placing check marks on the calendar and walking around the house trying out different names for the dog. Much to Rick's surprise, he doesn't miss a day the next week either.

Dinners are suddenly far more pleasurable. Michael occasionally mentions that he had to leave a game early; Rick nods sympathetically, and Michael lets it go with a shrug. He spends a lot of time speaking with great animation about the pluses and minuses of different breeds. No longer sitting in a fog of resentment, he also is able to hear his mother (a pharmacist) talk about such interesting topics as the latest controversy over a new drug. Michael is fascinated. Rick smiles. He and his wife can bring home the world to Michael, if he would just be *there*.

Well into the third week, Rick turns to the yellow pages to start making a list of animal shelters.

CHAPTER SIX

"I Can't Fall Asleep!"

OVERCOMING SLEEP PROBLEMS

Everyone needs a good night's sleep.

The problem is, it's not something you can legislate. If your child isn't sleeping well, neither will you. Sleep problems are among the most challenging of child-rearing difficulties. For one thing, they arise at the very time parents are least in the mood to deal with problems. The evening is a time to unwind and relax . . . not spend hours walking your child back into his room, or lying on his bed until you can hear his even breathing, or sitting in the rocker nodding out yourself until your child calls out, eyes closed, "You still there?" jolting you into a heart-pumping hyperawake state.

And that's assuming the problems appear only at bedtime. There's also the middle-of-the-night variety. You're enjoying a restful sleep, when suddenly an unfamiliar stirring awakens you to a tearful child slipping as quietly as possible under the covers of your bed. Or you're in the middle of the most delicious dream, only to be shocked into wakefulness by a child's piercing "Mommy! Come here!" Another poor night's sleep . . . at least for you.

So what should you do? Parents often feel torn. Do your children truly need your company to deal with nighttime fears? Or should you be striving to help your children develop independent ways of self-soothing?

Experts are split on this. At one extreme are those who think it's a high priority for children to learn to go to sleep on their own. At the other extreme are those who believe it's usually fine for children to have their parents' company as long as they need the succor. I myself think the truth lies somewhere in the middle and that when and how you assert your rules should depend on what is going on in your child's life.

Because there is sometimes a significant emotional component to sleep problems, it is wise to try and sort out what might be happening. Nighttime fears can be very powerful and often need to be discussed. Obviously, any major stress such as a death in the family or divorce can render a child terrified to be alone in her room. You will likely want to give your child all of the closeness she needs, especially when things are new and painful.

Less disturbing stressors can also cause nighttime anxiety. If one day your 5-year-old encounters a large barking dog off its leash, he may be haunted by memories when attempting to close his eyes that evening. Sitting with your child as he falls asleep or responding to his cries in the middle of the night would be an appropriate response to his fears.

However, if you give your child the nighttime attention she deserves, after a while she will probably get used to it and begin to feel she needs it even after the outside problem or crisis has passed. A child who clings to you out of habit needs to relearn her own ability to fall asleep, but she still deserves your patience and understanding. She might genuinely fear that if you leave her room too soon, she'll go back to sleepless nights. Here you can reassure her. "You know, for a few months I think you really needed me to stay with you. When Daddy left the house, you must have felt pretty scared. But you can see we are going to manage, and you do need to remember how to fall asleep on your own again. And I think I have a way to help you" would do nicely.

Finally, there are bedtime struggles more common to older children. They're not afraid to go to sleep; they simply don't want to part with the day or with the ongoing household activity. Sometimes power struggles are the root cause, and other times children have drifted into schedules that don't give them the rest they need.

CONQUERING NIGHTTIME FEARS

Five-year-old Heather is waking up every night and running into the bedroom of her parents Elizabeth and Bob. "I'm scared," Heather proclaims, lower lip quivering. "I am." She says this as if she expects an argument. Heather has always been an anxious child, and now she insists that she cannot go back to her room unless either Elizabeth or Bob comes and sits on her bed while she falls asleep. "Pleeeeze," she begs.

This pattern began 2 months earlier, when Heather had been experienc-

This chapter includes an in-depth sample Reward Plan for
• an anxious 5-year-old girl who wakes nightly,
plus briefer plans for
• a 3-year-old boy who refuses to move from his crib to a bed and
• a 10-year-old boy who resists getting to bed on time.

ing nightmares. One in particular about a witch who hovered outside her window had terrorized her. These nightmares followed news of a nighttime break-in at a house down the street. Fortunately, Heather seems to have forgotten about the break-in and is no longer having nightmares. Unfortunately, however, she is still waking up nightly. The pattern seems set.

Elizabeth and Bob have been taking turns sitting up with Heather, and the sleep disruption is unraveling both of them. They both instinctively feel that Heather is capable of sleeping through the night. However, she seems to have lost confidence in her ability to do so. Whenever they have tried to insist she stay in bed, tears ensue.

"I caaaaaan't," she wails whenever either of them says, "Heather, go back to bed yourself."

And so one or the other keeps vigil over Heather until her even breathing lets them know it's safe to go back to bed . . . although, more often than not, to toss and turn rather than find satisfying sleep themselves.

★ First, Talking About It ★

Heather has gotten up unusually late one Saturday morning, after having called for her mother twice during the night. She's rested. Unlike Elizabeth and Bob, Heather seems blissfully unaware of the frustration and anger she stirred up only hours ago.

Heather's parents decide this is a good time to try and get Heather talking.

"Honey," Elizabeth begins. "You wake up every night and say you're scared. What is it exactly you're so afraid of?"

Heather shrugs. "The witch maybe. Bad guys . . ." She says this quietly, without a lot of conviction.

Elizabeth nods. "Nighttime is the time when scary thoughts come for a visit." Elizabeth says this absolutely. "But Heather, you know you are perfectly safe in our house. We've showed you the way the windows lock and our front door is chained, and we even have an alarm! No one could ever get into our house."

Heather sighs. "You don't know that. I'm still scared."

"Yes, I see," Elizabeth nods, realizing that reality has nothing to do with this. "But you know, before you had those nightmares, you fell asleep just fine on your own."

"No, I never did, and I can't now!" Heather insists loudly. She gets where this is going, and she most definitely doesn't like it.

Rather than getting into an argument about whether or not she truly used to be able to stay by herself all night, Bob decides just to talk about the present situation. "Well, I know you feel you can't now, but your mother and I are impressed at how grown-up you're seeming during the day. You've even learned to ride a bike; you were scared when you first started. Remember? You go so fast now!"

Heather's scowl turns into a slight smile as she thinks about her biking accomplishments.

"We know you feel unhappy being alone at night," Bob says, purposefully getting Heather away from the word "scared." "But you know, big girls who can ride bikes can also go to asleep alone." Elizabeth and Bob smile reassuringly.

Heather opens her mouth to protest.

"Of course, sometimes they need a fun plan to help them learn to fall asleep," Elizabeth quickly adds, "a plan that also helps them chase away any unhappy thoughts."

"Like what?" Heather asks tentatively.

★ THE REWARD PLAN ★

Elizabeth and Bob decide that they will need a plan that provides very attractive, immediately available rewards. Heather's bedtime behavior is entrenched. Her parents want to see improvement from the get-go. They choose the Treasure Hunt chart (for a ready-to-use one, see the Pull-Out section at the back of the book) and prepare to use this chart by purchasing a number of small but enticing items that will appeal to Heather. (An illustration of this chart in use can be found on p. 125 in Part 3.)

Elizabeth begins by telling Heather that they have a plan to help her start falling asleep alone and that it will include a chance for her to go treasure hunting. It's a step-by-step plan, Elizabeth adds, so that Heather can feel safe and slowly get used to being alone. The last thing Elizabeth needs is for her to be scared that her parents expect too much of her.

Bob shows Heather the chart and explains that each night Heather is able to follow along with the "Sleeping On My Own" plan, the next morning she gets to search for a small "treasure." Bob calls this plan "Sleeping On My Own" because it sounds grown-up. "Sleeping Alone Plan" might have underlined what Heather is most afraid of.

Then Elizabeth outlines what they expect of Heather but explains that they will repeat each new step when the time comes. Heather is agreeable with her mother's words, but Elizabeth realizes that it's all very conceptual right now and that Heather's reaction will be quite different when she has to actually change her behavior.

★ WHAT HAPPENS ★

Bob and Elizabeth's plan includes five steps that require Heather to slowly wean herself of an adult's companionship in the middle of the night.

Step 1 (Nights 1–3)

For the first three nights, Heather must call for her parents instead of coming into their bedroom. One of her parents will come, Elizabeth assures her, but Heather must not leave her bedroom. If she manages to stay in her room, Heather will earn the opportunity to solve one clue and find a treasure!

The first night Heather forgets and enters her parents' bedroom. Bob reminds her of the plan. Bob and Elizabeth agree that this time, if she goes back to bed and calls out, she can earn the reward. Heather's parents feel

The sample plan that follows is designed to meet the needs of an anxious child. Many children will master their fears more quickly than Heather, and the slow steps of this plan may not be necessary. As always, adjust each program to your child's age and personality.

that allowing one night of "practice" may help Heather remember the next night. Also, they want Heather to feel successful from the outset of the plan.

At bedtime the next night, Elizabeth reminds Heather of the plan and tells her that she will get her reward only if she does not come into her parents' room. Heather worries that she won't remember when she wakes up in the middle of the night to stay in her room, and so together Elizabeth and Heather decide to place a brightly painted stool in the open doorway to Heather's room next to the night-light. Heather puts her favorite doll on it so that it looks like a "friendly seat." Heather earns a reward that night and the following night as well.

Step 2 (Nights 4–6)

Elizabeth and Bob explain to Heather that on the next three nights, if and when Heather calls out, Heather has to allow her mother or father to sit on a chair next to the bed, rather than on the bed. Heather agrees to this plan when her parents explain it to her late that afternoon, but in the middle of the night she insists that Bob (whose turn it is tonight) must sit on the bed. He reminds her of the plan and sits instead in the chair.

This proves to be the hardest night of the entire program. Reality is kicking in for Heather. Seismic changes (as she sees it) are expected. Heather begins to tantrum, wailing that she is too scared and cannot possibly fall asleep without someone on her bed. Her father considers giving in to her demands and simply withholding the reward the following morning, but he is unsure how that will make things any different the following night. He decides that Heather will progress faster if she is pushed a little to master her fears.

While Heather is crying, Bob suggests that there must be ways for her to help herself feel more secure. He places a doll under one arm and her assortment of bears at the foot of her bed. After 5 minutes of crying, Heather sees that her father is still sitting quietly and patiently by her bed. He whispers, "You're doing great!" Eventually she falls asleep.

In the morning, Elizabeth congratulates Heather and tells her how proud she is that she managed to fall asleep without someone on the bed. Once again, Heather gets to go on the treasure hunt, and this time she earns a particularly attractive item.

Heather is able to fall asleep with one of her parents sitting on a chair in her room for the next two nights.

Step 3 (Nights 7–16)

Elizabeth and Bob continue the plan over the next 10 days, slowly moving the chair further from Heather's bed and toward their bedroom. Elizabeth and Bob sit in the same spot several nights in a row before moving the chair farther away to minimize Heather's discomfort and sense of being rushed. Heather protests each time the chair is moved, but after the first night she seems to grow accustomed to the distance.

During this process, Heather occasionally forgets and comes into her parents' bedroom. When reminded of the plan, she allows herself to be walked back to her room, and one of her parents then sits in the chair as planned. The next morning Heather accepts the fact that she does not get a reward and thinks about how to remind herself the next night. Heather remembers the painted stool and asks Elizabeth to remind her to place it in the doorway at bedtime. She starts to talk about the treasure hunt when going to bed, and it seems clear to her parents that she is using it to motivate and comfort herself. During the day, she speaks proudly of her accomplishments.

Steps 4 and 5 (Nights 17–24)

By the time Heather has earned 15 rewards, Elizabeth and Bob have moved the chair to the entrance to their bedroom. At this point, they tell Heather that she will get to go on the treasure hunt only if she calls out to her parents and they call back but do not have to get out of bed.

Finally, Bob and Elizabeth require that Heather not call out at all. This scares her a little. Elizabeth promptly discusses new ways that Heather might comfort herself. Heather suggests that Elizabeth put a new fun night-light in her room. The one she has is kind of "boring." She's seen one in the shape of a smiling moon—that would make her feel happy, she says. Elizabeth gets her the new night-light. Heather manages this final step and earns the last of the 24 treasures.

★ THE INVISIBLE REWARDS ★

Heather is so proud of her ability to "sleep like a big girl." Her parents had been worried that she would continually want rewards to stay in bed, but in fact Heather views the plan as a kind of journey that she has undertaken successfully. It had a beginning, middle, and end. And according to Heather, well, she won! Bob awards her an "I Did It!" Certificate (for a blank one, see the Pull-Out section at the back of the book) to emphasize her achievement. Heather colors the certificate and tapes it to the wall above her bed. Heather brings up the treasure hunt again 5 months later, when Elizabeth is frustrated over Heather's fear of swimming. Heather cannot recall what behavior was rewarded when they last used the plan, but she remembers it was a fun way to overcome a problem.

★ ALSO WORKS FOR . . . ★

This step-by-step process for helping your child face a fear also works well for such classic childhood dreads as

- learning to swim,
- approaching dogs, and
- going into darkened rooms.

The critical thing to keep in mind is not to push too hard too quickly and to have a reward waiting in the wings every step of the way. A fear is hard to move past. Knowing that a "prize" is just around the corner can help give most children the courage they need to inch forward. Just don't look for giant steps!

ACCEPTING THE NEW BED

Three-year-old Carlos is quite content with his crib. He has not once asked for a "big boy bed." Still, a new baby is 3 months away, and so his mother Sofia buys him a twin bed.

"Look!" Sofia exclaims. "You're old enough to sleep in a big bed!"

Carlos ignores the compliment. He's not pleased at all. "I want to sleep in my bed!" he snaps. *"No!"*

Sofia tries to reason with him, flatter him, cajole him. "You're getting to be such a big boy!" she says admiringly. "You can do so many things now! Come, give it a try! Just lie down on this nice new bed for a few minutes."

Carlos shakes his head emphatically.

Sofia can't exactly say she's surprised by Carlos's resistance. Carlos has never adapted easily to change. To this day, the only lollipops he's ever had are red. The thought of what it's going to be like when the new baby appears on the scene gives her pause.

For a fleeting moment, Sofia wonders where she can hide the infant.

The quandary passes. Her newborn will need that crib, and it is time for Carlos to find his way into the new bed.

★ FIRST, TALKING ABOUT IT ★

Given Carlos's young age, Sofia realizes that a verbal discussion is not likely to prove helpful. Carlos clearly is not ready to begin to talk rationally about the new bed, and furthermore, pointing out that the crib will be given to the new baby would only make him more attached to it. With 3 months to wait, she may not need to make an issue about the reason for the move to the new bed. However, Sophia realizes she can help Carlos begin to process his feelings about the change in sleeping space without actually talking about it.

Even though space is tight, Sofia decides to leave the crib in the room and allow him to sleep there and to begin by simply helping him get used to the new bed's presence. For a few nights, she sits on the bed without comment and reads him his bedtime stories. She then tucks in a few of his stuffed animals and kisses them goodnight. By now, Carlos has stopped complaining about the new bed's presence in his room and seems to see it as a friendly fixture.

★ THE REWARD PLAN ★

Now Sofia moves into reward mode. She knows that Carlos is fascinated by animals of all kinds. She has chosen the Welcome to the Zoo chart (for a ready-to-

use one, see the Pull-Out section) and has already purchased some zoo animal stickers. She shows these stickers to Carlos and tells him that he can earn the opportunity to get a sticker and place it on the Zoo chart each night that he falls asleep in his new bed. After earning seven stickers, Dad will take him on a trip to the zoo. Carlos looks through the stickers and is immediately interested.

To help Carlos keep track of his progress toward earning the trip to the zoo, his mother brings out a Picture Contract. (An illustration of his Picture Contract in use can be found on p. 130 in Part 3.) In the upper half, labeled "ME!" she sketches a picture of Carlos sleeping in his new bed, his favorite bunny rabbit by his side. Then, she draws seven circles and explains to Carlos he can color in a circle every time he earns a sticker. She tells Carlos that after all the circles are colored, he'll be able to head for the zoo! In the "YOU!" section of the contract, she sketches Dad and Carlos holding hands, looking at a giraffe. Carlos "counts" the circles: "1...2...4...5...3...6...7!" His

Welcome to the Zoo Chart

mother smiles approvingly; he's got the right idea, which is what matters. And his counting is about as good as her sketch!

Next, she hangs the chart above the new bed. Carlos can't take his eyes off it.

★ WHAT HAPPENS ★

That night he hunkers down under the covers without an argument, surrounded by his stuffed animals. The next night too. The third night, he starts to balk at getting into the big bed, but Sofia is ready. She acts dismayed, commenting, "I can't fit into the crib to read this new panda bear book I have for you!" Carlos immediately forgets to fuss, keeping his eyes on the cover of the new book. Sofia sits down on the bed and begins to read. Distracted by the surprise, Carlos settles in.

ACCEPTING BEDTIME RULES

Ten-year-old Eric has always been very resistant to going to bed. He dawdles endlessly, going on last-minute hunts for missing library books, suddenly remembering phantom assignments that must get done, and complaining that he's simply not tired. It has not escaped Trish, his mother, that much of this problem is her fault. She had been a single mother for many years, and Eric had been able to squeak by with a number of behaviors she might not have tolerated had she been less tired and thus able to put her foot down. But now that she has remarried, Eric's inappropriate nocturnal habits are standing out in bold relief. In fact, they seem to be getting worse. Trish's new husband feels that 10 p.m. is late enough for Eric to be bustling about, and she agrees with him. Every evening, as the "witching hour" approaches, the tension in the house begins to thicken.

★ FIRST, TALKING ABOUT IT ★

One evening, when Eric's stepfather is not around, Trish sits down with her son and asks him if he's noticed how unhappy everyone gets around the time he's due to go to bed. He nods with a sour look on his face, and so Trish moves to a clearly empathic stance. "I'm wondering," she begins, "if you think somehow that me telling you it's time for bed means I don't want you around?" Eric shrugs, and so Trish continues by explaining that in the past she had made a mistake by letting him stay up so late. "I do enjoy your company, but I think you need more sleep than you've been getting." She reminds him of how hard it is for him to get up in the morning.

Trish then approaches the Reward Plan by saying, "I think that we should decide on something you and I can do together—kind of like a tradition—in the evening before bedtime." They used to do this when he was younger, but somehow as he got older and Trish started dating more, those special moments had fallen by the wayside. It strikes Trish that reinstating special private time might help Eric. She suggests a game of checkers. Eric doesn't argue; Trish takes this for a yes. Buoyed by the idea that he might respond to an outside motivation, Trish presents her Reward Plan.

★ THE REWARD PLAN ★

"I have an idea that will help you climb into bed more easily," she begins. "It ends with a day at your favorite amusement park."

Eric perks up.

Trish proposes the following goals: At 8:30 p.m. Eric will review with her the things he needs to remember for school. He'll pack everything up. Trish will then play a game of checkers with him. At 9:15 Eric will begin to prepare for bed. He'll change into his sleepwear, brush his teeth, choose a book or magazine to read, or find a sketch pad and pencil. He will put them next to his bed. At 9:45 Eric will read or draw to relax, and then he will turn off the lights at 10 p.m.

Eric bristles at the timetable, but he quickly quiets down when Trish suggests that he can make a small adjustment. He wants to turn off the lights at 10:15. It's a move for some control, she realizes. It also doesn't really matter.

"When do we go to Cyclone City?" Eric asks. Trish explains the details.

Together Trish and Eric prepare two Keeping Track charts with the three times and tasks heading the first, second, and third columns on each one. (Two charts will be needed to accommodate the 20 days to be included in the plan; an illustration of one of these charts in use can be found on p. 123 in Part 3.) Then at the left side of each chart's first column of lines, they list the weekdays for the next month (10 days per chart). Each time Eric completes a bedtime routine task on time, he gets a check mark on the corresponding line. Trish explains that if Eric can earn 55 check marks in the next month, (missing only 5 opportunities), he's got a trip to Cyclone City in the bag.

★ WHAT HAPPENS ★

Trish and her husband are amazed at the immediate change in Eric's evening behavior. Eric decides to set his wrist alarm for 8:20 p.m. to warn him it's almost time to pack up for school. He has no trouble being ready for the checkers game, bringing the checkers set out and setting it up before Trish even comes into the den. And despite Eric's insistence that he be able to stay awake until 10:15 p.m., Trish notices his light is often out at 10:00. Trish realizes she was probably right to suspect that Eric's earlier procrastination had had something to do with jealous feelings towards his stepfather and his having had a sense that he had become less important to his mother.

Trish thinks ahead to the amusement park trip, imagining the pride that Eric will feel when he and his stepfather step off the roller coaster together. Secretly, she's hoping that this trip will give Eric an opportunity to build a stronger bond with his stepfather. It will also provide an opportunity for the three of them to do something that centers on Eric and for him to feel like the star of the show. These will be his invisible rewards.

But Trish will also get an invisible reward. Eric will have gone for his first roller coaster ride with an enthusiastic escort, and *she* will have stayed safely on the ground!

"No Shampoo Tonight!"

ESTABLISHING HASSLE-FREE HYGIENE

A good many children lack any interest in cleanliness. In fact, children generally view hygiene activities as a nuisance. Why take a bath, or shampoo their hair, or brush their teeth, when there are so many other things to do? Especially if these tasks forestall dinner or prevent them from going straight to bed for their evening story or mean they have to put a little brush in their mouth and listen to you chant, "Up, down, right, left!" They are probably thinking to themselves, What's all this fuss about?

The idea that dirt under the fingernails can introduce germs, that filthy hair is unattractive, or that unbrushed teeth can invite cavities simply fails to spark the faintest interest.

Dirt rules.

As a parent, you need to recognize that it will take time for your child to respond to your explanations about why it's so important to pay attention to hygiene. It's unrealistic to expect that what you say about it will have a lot of impact while she is young. The information (some of it) will only slowly seep into her brain, and as time goes by and she grows older, her own desire to feel clean and to be attractive to others will mesh with your words of wisdom. Suddenly, taking a bath, shampooing, and brushing teeth (among other things) will make sense.

But that's then, and this is now.

The success of the Reward Plans outlined in this chapter will depend almost entirely on the degree to which they are attractive to your child. Your child will not go along with you because he has some untapped desire to be clean. But he usually will have some sense that this is part of your protecting and taking care of him. And when they're not into seeking control, children typically have some willingness to cooperate.

But hygiene demands often arise when children are tired, hungry, or in a hurry. These are not the times they're most open to acquiring new habits! And although it's true that children won't, for the most part, be getting in touch with the invisible rewards associated with good hygiene right now, when the invisible rewards do kick in over time, this process will have helped get them there. The immediate rewards you offer are a temporary measure that will help change your child's unhealthy habits to healthy ones in ways that bring pleasure, not pain. And again, you'll be safeguarding a positive relationship between you and your child.

This chapter provides an in-depth sample Reward Plan for
- a 3-year-old girl who resists nightly toothbrushing,
plus briefer plans for
- a 6-year-old girl who hates having her hair washed and
- a 10-year-old boy who comes to the dinner table with a dirty face and hands.

TIME TO BRUSH TEETH!

Three-year-old Sara puts up a struggle each evening when her mother Sam attempts to brush her teeth. Sam has experimented with having her do some of it herself ("Aren't you a big girl!"), but it doesn't hold much attraction. Sara does not like the feel of the brush in her mouth, whether it's in her hand or Sam's.

Sam has tried gentle coaxing, such as, "Come Sara. Let's you and I do it together," but Sara usually replies, "No fanks." So now, sometimes Sam doesn't bother at all. She makes excuses to herself. "She hasn't had a cavity yet, and we're only talkin' baby teeth," she thinks to herself.

She's also at times resorted to threats, such as throwing out all the cookies in the house, but Sara just wailed "Noooo! I want cookies!" and then clamped her lips together so tight nothing could have pried them open.

Half the time, Sam would rather go to the dentist herself than deal with Sara.

★ FIRST, TALKING ABOUT IT ★

Sam knows she can't expect a very young child to get the concept of cleaning teeth to avoid decay. However, she decides to periodically explain the purpose of brushing anyway in the simplest of terms. "Sara, it's not good for your teeth to have food left on them. They need to be cleaned up like the rest of you. If you don't take care of them, they can start to hurt!" (After your child has his first cavity, the tide may turn slightly, but even then it will depend on age.)

For now it seems wise to be sympathetic and to focus on other aspects of the toothbrushing experience. "I know you don't like the way the brush feels, but maybe we can do something to make it more comfortable. We could go to the drugstore and pick out a new toothbrush that's very soft, and you can get one in your favorite color! Also, before we start brushing, we can wipe your teeth with a soft, warm washcloth. That will help your mouth get ready for brushing."

"OK," Sara says, a little tentatively. She's uncertain. Not a pushover, Sam muses to herself with a little pride.

Basically, Sam is showing her child in concrete terms that she wants to make the experience better for her in whatever way she can. Once home from the drugstore, she says to Sara, "I know something else we can do to make toothbrushing more fun. We'll call it 'Brushing to Help Feed Kitty!'" Sam knows Sara adores cats, and so as anticipated, she has her complete attention.

"What?" Sara says, eyes wide.

★ THE REWARD PLAN ★

The following Reward Plan is appropriate for young children. Older children can be given rewards not just for brushing their teeth but for spending a sufficient amount of time on the task. If your older child tends to do rush jobs that miss the remnants of that day's munching, you can set a timer and reward her for spending 2 or 3 minutes brushing her teeth. You can also expect that she can wait longer for her reward!

Because Sam anticipates that the struggle to get Sara's teeth cleaned carefully will be an ongoing one for at least a few months, she has devised a variety of plans to capture Sara's interest and gain her cooperation. She knows that Sara maintains interest in any particular activity for only short periods of time. She begins by showing Sara the Feed the Kitty chart (see the Pull-Out section at the back of the book) and explains to Sara that each time she allows Sam to brush her teeth, or starts herself and then lets Sam finish, Sara will earn a food sticker that she can place in the cat's dish. (An example of this chart with stickers affixed can be found on p. 124 in Part 3.) Sam suggests that Sara choose a name for the cat, and after some deliberation she decides on "Tiger." Then Sam shows her the collection of stickers she has purchased: Sara can earn a variety of foods for Tiger, ranging from veggies to candy to hamburgers! Sam hangs the chart in Sara's room above her bed so that Tiger can keep her company at night.

The first night Sara chooses an ice cream cone for Tiger, and Sam and she laugh at the idea of a cat eating a cone. On subsequent evenings, Tiger is fed many different foods. Sometimes Sam encourages Sara to feed Tiger something healthy and good for her teeth!

As Sara brushes her teeth and puts stickers on the chart, Sam occasionally talks about the grooming habits of cats. At times through the day, Sam sees Sara watching with intense interest as Alice, the family cat, grooms herself.

However, as with most 3-year-olds, Sara's enthusiasm begins to fade as her short attention span peters out. Because the Feed the Kitty chart is losing its luster, Sara begins to balk (but maybe a tad less than before) when it's time to brush her teeth. Still, Sam is thrilled. Sara has been brushing for almost 2 weeks! It's apparent that the right outside motivator can be quite effective, and so without letting any significant time lapse so that Sara is once again standing with lips cemented shut, Sam introduces Happy Tokens (for blank ones, see the Pull-Out section).

Sitting down with Sara, Sam shows her several Happy Token shapes and explains that Sara will collect one each time she brushes her teeth. The first night, Sara opts for a star. Sam hands her a small box that she has already wrapped in plain paper. Sam suggests that Sara decorate the box, which is going to be her token holder. As Sara plays along, making squiggle lines with crayons, Sam explains that she will get a token each time she brushes her teeth. On the back of each token Sam writes, "Yes! I brushed today!"

Sara is back to brushing with a minor vengeance (she doesn't like it if Sam's part takes too long) and soon has a boxful of tokens. She has decorated each token using crayons and stickers. Sara's been brushing regularly for almost 3 weeks! A few times Sam has caught her rewarding her dolls with tokens for some imagined good turn.

Again, however, as is to be expected, Sara tires of the tokens. She's still brushing but is starting to argue, and Sam notices the token box lying idle under her bed. Time for something new.

Sam turns to what she calls the Pop Bead Reward Plan. She gives Sara a short string of beads to begin with. Each night after toothbrushing, Sara can select a new bead to add to the chain. The goal is to make a string of beads long enough to form a necklace. And that's exactly as long as this plan lasts. Sara's good for the jewelry, but as soon as the necklace fits, she starts looking at the toothbrush cross-eyed. She keeps brushing though. Sort of. Even though she's not exactly enjoying it, the habit is forming.

The Activity Treats (see the Pull-Out section) are next. Sam selects activities that would most appeal to Sara, writes them on the forms, and cuts out the slips of paper. She explains to Sara that every time she brushes her teeth, she gets to pick a slip of paper out of a bag. Each paper promises a special activity the two of them can do together. Sara asks, "What you mean?" so Sam gives her a few examples, including Get a Ribbon Braid in Your Hair, Learn a New Dance, Make a Puzzle, and Ask Mom to Sing Her Favorite Song. She's in.

Finally, there are the Silly Toothbrushing Songs. Sara's dad makes an audiotape of himself singing amusing songs about toothbrushing. She laughs hysterically when Sam plays it for her. Sam then explains that Sara can listen to a different song each time she brushes her teeth. Music to brush by!

Example (sung to the tune of "The Ants Go Marching Two by Two"):

The toothbrush goes brushing two by two, hurrah!
    Hurrah!
The toothbrush goes brushing two by two, hurrah!
    Hurrah!
The toothbrush goes brushing two by two,
The little one stops to pick up a cracker crumb,
And they all go brushing down, and around, and
    under the tongue,
Boom, boom, boom...

★ THE INVISIBLE REWARDS ★

When it comes to hygiene, the invisible rewards are mainly yours. Sam discovers that after a couple of months, Sara cooperates much more readily with toothbrushing, even as she grows bored with the incentives. Cooperation is becoming a habit. Sam doesn't have to argue with her as much and can feel good that she's found a way for Sara to have healthy teeth and gums. Also she's pleased that the dentist bills stay modest!

Sara will not come to appreciate the invisible reward until she is much older. Even then, she probably won't thank her mom. As a teenager, she'll be too busy arguing with her about other things, such as "that dumb curfew." But as she marches indignantly into the bathroom to brush her teeth before bed, Sam will have at least something to smile about.

★ ALSO WORKS FOR . . . ★

A succession of different Reward Plans offering modest incentives for young children works well when they are resisting something that is relatively benign and something you need them to do on a daily (or almost) basis. Your children will play along with your plan as long as it shines brightly enough to smother their annoyance. As the glow diminishes, their impatience will take center stage once more, and so you need to be ready with another Reward Plan until your child has been at the new good habit long enough for it to become, well, habit! This kind of succession of simple plans will work well for behaviors such as

- wiping well after going to the bathroom,

- washing hands after toileting,
- flossing teeth, and
- taking medication.

SHAMPOOING ON SCHEDULE

Maria's 6-year-old daughter Elisa abhors having her hair washed. "My eyes!" she always screams. "Get the soap out of my eyes!" Then there's the issue of temperature. The water is either too cold or too hot (when it's basically tepid) and even sometimes *"too wet!"* And finally comes the struggle to comb the tangles out of Elisa's long hair. "You're pulling all my hair out!" Elisa wails. The entire shampoo experience has turned into a time-consuming battleground.

During the winter months, Maria had no quarrel with Elisa going a few days between shampoos. However, it's the summer now. Elisa is an active girl who spends a lot of time running around on dusty playgrounds and splashing in chlorinated pools. Maria feels she needs to shampoo almost every day. Unfortunately, Elisa is exhausted when she comes home from camp and has no tolerance for anything even slightly to her disliking, and when Maria reaches for the shampoo bottle, Elisa practically catapults herself out of the tub.

Elisa has always been a bit sensitive to sensations, especially tactile ones. T-shirts have to feel like butter. Sock seams have to be straight. Collars chafe her, and anything but sweatpants is a no-no. Maria has to admit that it isn't shocking that the experience of water spilling down her face would make Elisa apoplectic.

Still, she needs the shampoos, and Maria feels that if she'd just give her a chance, they could be *very* quick. Maria could even find ways to help minimize the offending sensations if Elisa would just calm down. She decides that a tantalizing reward might just do the trick.

Elisa loves to somersault, stand on her head, and do other gymnastic feats. In fact, she frequently says she wants to win a gold medal at the Olympics. Maria decides to use this dream of hers to get her attention. She wants to suggest ways to make the shampooing easier and offer her something she wants very badly . . . and that Maria had been thinking about providing for her anyway. Gymnastics lessons.

★FIRST, TALKING ABOUT IT★

Maria waits for a day when Elisa comes home more proud of herself than exhausted. "I did a backwards somersault today!" she announces. Maria tells her how proud she is of her. "Can I take gymnastics lessons?" Elisa immediately asks.

"You know something, Elisa," Maria begins, "I think a gymnastics class is a great idea. I would like you to do that, but I'd really like to make a trade."

Elisa's face lights up, and Maria continues. "If you'll take a shampoo every day after camp for a straight week without struggling, I will enroll you in a class. And you can continue taking classes as long as you keep shampooing."

"Really?" she asks. "But do I have to wash my hair every day?" Maria can tell she's weighing things. And so she helps her along.

"But I'm not talking about the old way of shampooing. I think we can find ways to do it so you don't hate it as much. First of all, you can hold your head way back, and I can slowly pour water onto your hair until it's wet all over."

"Then I can work in the shampoo, and when I'm done you can lean back like you're doing a back float, and we can wash the shampoo out. If there's any soap left, you can lift your head slightly, and I'll use a cup to wash it out, but your head will be back so no water will get on your face." Maria has actually tried to do this with her before, but Elisa was thrashing around so much it never really helped. "And at the end, we'll work on a way to comb out your hair so it hardly pulls. I'll start at the ends and work up slowly, and I bet you'll only feel the tiniest of tugs."

"I don't know," Elisa mutters.

"We'll try it tonight," Maria says confidently. "You can decide."

The choice is in Elisa's hands. She doesn't feel cornered. In fact, Maria thinks she looks just a little hopeful. To sweeten things a bit, Maria volunteers that on rainy days when she plays inside, Elisa can skip a shampoo. Elisa's no fool and asks if it still counts as part of the week.

Maria is no fool either, and she says yes quickly and with a laugh.

★ THE REWARD PLAN ★

That evening Elisa calmly gets into the tub, and Maria talks her through what she's doing. It works almost perfectly. Elisa agrees to "the deal." To underline the seriousness of her offer of gymnastics lessons, Maria produces a Contract (for a blank one, see the Pull-Out section). Elisa is intrigued and asks what the Contract is for. Maria explains that when adults agree to a business deal, they usually sign a contract to clinch the deal and make sure each person keeps her side of the bargain. "Let's write down exactly what each of us agrees to do," Maria proposes.

She fills in the Contract. Both Maria and Elisa sign it, and Maria adds the date. To help Elisa keep track (and clearly see the reward growing closer and closer), Maria uses the Daily Checklist. (An example of a Daily

Checklist in use can be found on p. 123 in Part 3. For a blank one, see the Pull-Out section.)

★ WHAT HAPPENS ★

Elisa, other than showing a little body tension the first three days, is now much more cooperative. There isn't a single rainy day that week, and Elisa receives seven check marks. Maria expounds on what a big girl she is, and by the third week Elisa slips into the tub as easily as she leaps onto the trampoline!

WASHING AWAY THE DIRT

Ten-year-old Shaquon plays down and dirty. He's an active child who climbs trees, thrives on the baseball field, and loves riding his bike through puddles. When dinnertime comes, he's *very* dirty and *very* hungry. This is not a winning combination.

Patty has attempted to require Shaquon to wash his hands and face before dinner, but the fact is she works long hours and often arrives late for dinner with Shaquon and her husband Will. Will is a writer who works hard at home, is frequently preoccupied, and is not nearly as distressed as Patty about Shaquon's dirty hands and face. In fact, he hardly seems to notice. When he does, he usually offhandedly suggests to Shaquon that he clean up and is easily satisfied with a perfunctory two seconds under the faucet and a quick-shake-dry kind of affair.

When Patty arrives home, tired and frazzled from her long workday, the last thing she needs to see is Shaquon's dirty face and limbs at the kitchen table. Although she sometimes thinks she should be more appreciative that Will has made dinner and supervised Shaquon's after-school activities, Patty's usual first words are to chide first Shaquon, and then her husband for failing to get Shaquon to wash up. She cannot believe she's got two people in the house who don't seem to seriously grasp that it's neither healthy nor civilized to approach the dinnertable wearing the latest in dirt. "He's a boy!" her husband chuckles, perhaps indirectly communicating resentment about her unappreciative entrance. "We're like that!" Patty ends up feeling like the crotchety outsider.

★ FIRST, TALKING ABOUT IT ★

Patty decides that the first step in resolving this problem is to enlist Will's regular assistance. And to obtain his assistance, Patty realizes that she would do well to apologize for her nagging and express her appreciation for all that Will does do. After thinking the problem over carefully, Patty sits down with Will alone one evening. "I'm sorry that my first words at dinner are usually complaints about you and Shaquon. I would love to sit down and compliment you on the dinner you've prepared. But I have a hard time seeing past Shaquon's dirt." Will is definitely surprised at Patty's apology. In turn, he apologizes for failing to instill better habits in Shaquon. Patty suggests a

Reward Plan in which everyone has a goal. Patty will resist nagging, Will will supervise Shaquon's washing up before dinner, and Shaquon will cooperate in doing a thorough job.

★ THE REWARD PLAN ★

On Saturday morning, Patty and Will present the plan to Shaquon. Will starts: "You know, I'm starting to agree with your mother. You just cannot come to the table looking like a walking mound of Mother Earth." Shaquon looks at the two of them, surprised. He's not used to seeing this united front.

Patty enters the conversation. "Shaquon, you've got to work on washing up, but I have to work on something, too. I'm tired when I get home from work, but that doesn't mean I should start nagging you and your dad first thing. If you guys take care of the dirt, I'll work on being nicer at dinner. Maybe if we all work on our parts in this, we can figure out a reward for us all."

Shaquon is listening carefully. There's a slight smile playing across his lips.

Employing his creative self, Will comes up with the reward. "Two straight weeks of cleaning up before dinner," he says, "and we'll all go get ourselves ice cream sundaes at Dessert Heaven!"

A slight grin appears on Shaquon's face. "OK, I suppose we can do it," he says, attempting to hide his enthusiasm.

Patty takes down the kitchen calendar and draws a star on Saturday's date 2 weeks hence. "How about we put check marks on the calendar each night," Patty suggests, "to keep track of our progress?"

★ WHAT HAPPENS ★

Knowing that both he and his son tend toward absent-mindedness, Will decides to set his wrist watch for 5:45 p.m. to remind the two of them to get the washing job done. All throughout the next week, when Patty arrives home each day at 6:00, a clean and smiling Shaquon awaits her. Patty feels her fatigue lighten as she sits down to eat with her family, and rather than nagging, she smiles appreciatively at Will and Shaquon.

Patty is positively thrilled. Not only is her son learning to eat in a more healthful and civilized manner, but he's getting what he needs more than anything: two parents united in their efforts to help him develop better habits, a happier dinner hour, and some fun time relaxing with the two of them.

The reward system has helped all of them hit pay dirt.

"He Hit Me First!"

GETTING ALONG WITH SIBLINGS

One of the most disheartening problems faced by parents with two or more children is the constant strife between them. For one thing, it can be intolerable to live with the rancor. But on a more emotional level, it goes against the fantasy so many mothers and fathers hold dear of children growing up together, trusting and relying on each other. Sure, there would be arguments, but as the years went by, they would learn to support each other, hold each other up during tough times, and be each other's confidant.

Instead, many parents live with fits over broken crayons, battles over which toy belongs to whom, angry accusations that one child is loved more than the other, and the occasional wooden block lobbed dangerously close to a sibling's eye. It's a difficult letdown—not to mention harrowing.

Still, it needn't spell doom. The first important thing to keep in mind is that some teasing and even physical fighting are normal and expected between siblings. The second thing to consider is that there may be ways you are contributing unknowingly to their struggles and that you may be overlooking simple ways to ease tensions. This is not to say the friction is your fault, but rather you might be able to take the edge off more easily than you think. Children fight for many reasons:

- One child might think you go much easier on the other in terms of expectations. This may be so for any number of reasons—age, capabilities, temperament, and more. Still, you might try and find some way to relax your demands on the first child while stepping up the goals for the other. This could help them both!

- Children often have a difficult time believing that parents have enough love for both of them. You might indeed be spending more time with your younger child, who needs more supervision. Perhaps you need to make special time with the eldest child.

- Then, too, simple boredom can create friction. The children can't think of anything else to do, so they look to each other for a way of burning off energy. It might be time for you to either help them plan a joint activity or put them into separate rooms, each with her own project, such as tiles for one and puzzles for another.

- Your children may feel you take sides too quickly when stepping into an argument. It would be wise to listen to both sides before offering up anything close to a judgment or consequence. Older children are often blamed for arguments. But younger siblings can be quite hurtful, and their victims cannot always be expected to control themselves with full maturity.

- There may be tensions in the house that your children are acting out. Because some children would rather be the focus of trouble than have to endure listening to their parents fight or thinking about an illness or any other trouble in the family, you might need to talk with them about the problem and, if indicated, get them outside counseling.

- Finally, siblings may simply become accustomed to fighting with each other and thus fail to develop enjoyable ways to spend time together. It's just what they do. And although they might not enjoy it, they have no idea how to break the patterns. Reward Plans are especially useful on this score!

The design of your sibling-rivalry Reward Plan will depend on your children's ages. When one of your children is a toddler, your plan will need to focus more on the behavior of your older child and to encourage him to control his angry impulses and to seek you out if trouble is brewing. However, when the children are all over 3 years old, it is often best to include them equally in the Reward Plan. You simply have to structure the plan in a way that reduces competition. If one child earns a reward and the other one fails to do so, you may only be fanning the flames of sibling squabbling!

This chapter provides an in-depth sample Reward Plan for
- 8- and 6-year-old brothers who frequently fight, plus briefer plans for
- a 5-year-old girl who is rough with her 2-year-old brother and
- a pair of sisters, ages 10 and 9, who borrow each other's clothes without asking.

THE ONLY TIME THEY DON'T FIGHT IS WHEN THEY'RE SLEEPING

Eight-year-old Pat and 6-year-old Chris fight with each other constantly. The scripts of their conflicts are fairly predictable. Pat refuses to share his markers with Chris, which sends Chris into howls of rage. Of course, Chris only wants to draw spacemen just the way his brother does—a sincere form of flattery, but Pat doesn't see it this way. He views Chris's behavior as pure interference. Chris, hurt and resentful, sometimes retaliates by scribbling with his crayons on Pat's drawings. Pat breaks his crayons, calls Chris a baby, and occasionally slaps Chris. And on and on . . .

Then there's the vying for favored territory. Although Angela, their mother, has tried to make the TV room comfortable for both children, the simple truth (though hardly of any great note) is that one spot on the sofa is a bit closer to the TV screen. Pat thinks he owns the prime seat. After all, he always sat there when Chris was an infant and toddler. Invariably, Chris ends up sobbing on the floor.

Finally, there are the fights over shared toys, such as the large box overflowing with Legos. Theoretically, these building toys belong to both boys jointly. But somehow when they play together, each child wants the same spaceman with the red helmet, blue pants, and white shoes.

Sometimes the fights are verbal and other times physical. First come the accusations. Then the denials. Voices become high pitched. Then the screaming begins, followed by tears, and then someone gets slapped. Although Chris usually makes the first physical move, Pat is quick to retaliate. Angela often sends them both to their rooms and the open warfare stops for a while, but Pat holds grudges. Usually he plots a payback.

It's January now. Both boys are cooped up in the house for longer periods together, and the atmosphere in the house is becoming impossible. Pat is more and more frequently muttering, "I hate Chris." Angela's raising her voice too frequently, and once or twice last week she found herself slapping Chris after he struck Pat. This is not, she realizes, an acceptable example of modeling conflict resolution.

Something has to change.

★ First, Talking About It ★

Angela decides it would be wisest to speak with each boy separately. She is concerned that if she speaks with them together, they will spend the entire time blaming each other and not hear a word she has to say.

She approaches Pat first. "Pat," she begins, with a warm, nonaccusatory voice, "You and Chris have been fighting so much lately. I know that Chris makes you very angry, and I can understand why. It must be frustrating when he scribbles on your drawings. And I know you don't like it when he sits in your favorite spot on the sofa. You used to sit there all the time yourself."

Pat is looking at Angela with surprise. He's feeling, she can sense, understood. This, she knows, is a wonderful gift to him. She gives him another.

"And to make matters worse, I start yelling, and that's really not helpful. I'm supposed to know better!" She is including yourself in the problem because she wants to keep Pat's defenses down and also because there is some truth about her involvement.

"But you know, Chris really looks up to you so much. That's why he always wants to use your markers. He thinks you draw *so* well. He admires you."

"So he should just tell me that," Pat gripes.

"Well, younger brothers don't usually put those kinds of feelings into words. It's much easier for Chris to tell you when he's mad at you! But I have an idea of how to help solve some of these problems for all of us, and we'll talk about it over dinner," Angela says with a confident nod of her head.

Then she talks to Chris, again going for a nonaccusatory stance. "Chris, I know you haven't been having much fun with Pat lately. You want to use his markers so you can draw like him, but he doesn't want to share. You always feel pushed out of the best stuff, like that seat on the sofa. These kind of things can be hard to take."

"Pat's not so nice," Chris says somberly.

"I know sometimes he doesn't behave nicely. You boys aren't always kind to each other. You shouldn't hit each other. And guess what? Sometimes I don't behave well either. I slapped you! That's not right, either!"

Chris looks at Angela, surprised. "Yeah!"

"We're all not understanding and appreciating each other very well. But I have a plan to help. We'll discuss it over dessert after dinner."

To start off on a positive note, Angela brings out the boys' favorite ice cream pops after dinner (fortunately, they like the same ones). They both look quite relaxed, and so she begins.

"I have a plan for how the two of you can start having more fun together," she states. "I think I have a way to help you stop all this fighting and to put an end to my yelling also!"

"Wow, no more yelling," Chris says with a grin.

"Yes, I'll try my best," Angela laughs. "What I have in mind will take a little self-control for everybody, but there's going to be a reward at the end." Her tone is light. The boys are licking their pops. There's a present in sight. What could be bad?

She's on.

★ THE REWARD PLAN ★

Rather than giving each child a separate Reward Plan, which would contribute to feelings of competition and conflict, Angela decides to create a plan that requires the boys to cooperate. The children will form a team, and they will win or lose together. Thus, it is in *both* children's interest to behave well and to encourage each other to do so.

Angela chooses the Blue Lagoon chart (for a ready-to-use one, see the Pull-Out section at the back of the book) to record their progress. She explains that two rafts will race each other to their destinations, and both children will share the navigation of each raft. She then explains how the plan will work. One raft, named *Ocean Breeze*, will move forward one space when the boys do one of the following:

- take turns sitting in the favorite sofa spot for one day,
- use words rather than fists to express angry feelings,
- offer to share a toy (such as the markers!) with the other, or
- do a kind act for the other.

The other vehicle, *Ragged Raft*, will move forward one space each time
- either child hits the other,
- Chris scribbles on Patrick's drawing or breaks something of Patrick's, or
- Patrick calls Chris a baby or other hurtful name.

Because the Blue Lagoon chart is designed to put more emphasis on positive behaviors than negative ones, *Ocean Breeze* has a longer journey to travel. *Ocean Breeze* moves on the outer path of the chart, which has 30 spaces, whereas Ragged Raft travels only 12 spaces on the inner path. Angela explains that she will indicate the movement of the rafts by drawing an arrow across a space every time one of the boys does one of the behaviors she has listed. (An illustration of this chart in use can be found on p. 126 in Part 3.)

If *Ocean Breeze* reaches the Blue Lagoon before *Ragged Raft* gets to the Dismal Swamp, the boys will get to take a special bus trip to their favorite toy store, which has a large wall filled with small items such as puzzles, figures, and games. Each child will get $5 to spend. Angela decides on this reward because it will give the children a chance to participate in a shared activity that celebrates their accomplishments.

Pat notes, with some concern, that *Ocean Breeze* has a longer path to travel to its end point. Angela acknowledges this, but she tells the boys that the things they have to do to move *Ocean Breeze* ahead are very easy. They'll soon see she is right. All Pat has to do is offer to help Chris build a Lego car. All Chris has to do is to help Pat find a piece for his plane.

★ WHAT HAPPENS ★

Angela finishes explaining the rules of this plan as the boys are finishing up their ice cream bars. They are excited about the Blue Lagoon chart and the bus trip, and so Pat immediately offers Chris the opportunity to use his markers. Chris beams, and Angela happily compliments Pat and makes the first arrow on *Ocean Breeze*'s route.

Pat, clearly on a roll, suggests the boys play with Legos, and during the first 10 minutes each boy runs to the kitchen several times to tell his mother that he has shared a toy. Angela recognizes that this enthusiasm for the chart is unlikely to continue for too much longer, and so she continues to commend the boys and with great drama draws arrows to move *Ocean Breeze* along its path.

By the end of the first day, *Ocean Breeze* has moved eight spaces, and *Ragged Raft* hasn't budged from the starting point. During the next few days, the house is remarkably calm. Although positive behaviors seem to be waning (*Ocean Breeze* has now moved a total of 14 spaces), there have been few problems. *Ragged Raft* has advanced only four spaces, so *Ocean Breeze* is still ahead. Angela suggests, anticipating possible trouble, that the boys do something kind or helpful for the other just to keep *Ocean Breeze*'s sail ready to catch the wind. They laugh at that and then offer each other some toys to play with. Angela realizes that these acts don't, at the time they are performed, come from the heart, but there is a positive atmosphere in the home now and better feelings between the boys.

Then the inevitable happens. On the evening of the fourth day, Chris and Pat get into a couple of fights over toys. *Ragged Raft* gets to move ahead two spaces, and both boys begin to blame each other for its advance. Quickly, Angela tries to focus the boys on the opportunity for positive progress. "Are you going to just sit back and let *Ocean Breeze* drift in the water?" she challenges. They quickly respond by deciding to help each other clean up their room. *Ocean Breeze* gets a boost, and the boys forget about their fight.

The trouble isn't over, however. The next day Pat comes to Angela in tears, showing her a drawing Chris has scribbled on. She realizes that this is a delicate point in the plan. Although she will have to move *Ragged Raft* ahead one space, she doesn't want Pat to become so angry with Chris that the positive tone of the plan simply evaporates. She comforts Pat and tells him she's going to work with Chris to help him earn points for *Ocean Breeze*. She pulls Chris aside, who cries out, "Pat wouldn't let me use his markers!"

Angela says that she understands, but that ruining Pat's drawing isn't nice, and that perhaps he can move *Ocean Breeze* forward by drawing, with his crayons, a picture of apology for Pat. He draws a heart for Pat and *Ocean Breeze* moves forward, but she can see that Pat is still uptight.

As the boys are playing, Angela suddenly sees an opportunity to use the shaping technique. Pat, who decides to reach for a new toy, places the one he may still be interested in next to him. Chris immediately picks it up. Before Pat can say a word, Angela exclaims, "Pat!! How nice! You're sharing that toy with Chris! *Ocean Breeze* sails again!" Pat looks up with surprise, but then quickly smiles broadly.

As the days go by, Angela can see that the boys are learning it is in their interest to encourage good behaviors in each other and to even be more tolerant and helpful when one of them steps over the line. One afternoon, she actually hears Pat warning Chris not to hit him again because he will be "helping *Ragged Raft* out!" Because Pat did not report Chris's hitting to her, Angela decides not to count it. The boys have indeed been trying, and she wants to be certain the plan ends on a positive note.

★ THE INVISIBLE REWARDS ★

After they earn the reward, the boys' behavior continues to be considerably friendlier than before the Reward Plan. Although the fighting resumes somewhat, the children's interaction remains much improved for a number of weeks. Angela has helped them break a pattern of destructive behavior in which they had gotten unhappily stuck.

Pat and Chris have learned an interesting lesson in compromise as well. In late February, after a big snowfall, when the boys are arguing over who sits where on the sled, Pat suggests they make a snow chart for turn

taking, and Chris immediately agrees. Using a broken stick, he creates one on the snow!

Angela knows they haven't eliminated sibling rivalry forever. But there are more good feelings around now. The boys have had an extended experience of enjoying each other's company. Angela feels that she has contributed to a foundation that will make it more likely the boys will be close when they grow older. And she is feeling like a parent in control. Rather than feeling guilty about losing her temper with the boys, she feels proud that she has found a way to help them enjoy each other.

★ ALSO WORKS FOR . . . ★

A Reward Plan that requires easy but frequent good behaviors and penalizes the least tolerable behaviors can break unhappy patterns. This kind of plan provides an engaging way of limiting negative behaviors and at the same time encourages positive ones. The Blue Lagoon chart can be used to track the positive and negative behaviors of a single child as well as of two or more children. The challenge isn't hard, the success is quick, and the penalties included in the chart serve as a gentle reminder to stay on track. This kind of plan would work well for behaviors such as

- using appropriate language rather than swearing,
- showing good manners rather than poor ones, and
- wearing a safety helmet when biking or rollerblading rather than going bareheaded.

HELPING THE OLDER SIBLING FIND A ROLE THAT WORKS

Five-year-old Katie claims she loves her 2-year-old brother Johnny. She just can't take her hands off of him. She likes to grab him and give him a big, hard hug or carry him around in an awkward position (for him), or just kind of toss him on her bed with not-such-merry abandon. "I love Johnny!" she says gleefully. Katie also revels in "teaching Johnny lessons" when he tries to do things she knows her mom, Allison, doesn't allow. If he tries to climb up on the kitchen stools, Katie shouts "No!" and pulls him down roughly.

Repeatedly, Allison has asked Katie to be more gentle. She's told her she might accidentally drop Johnny. And she's asked Katie to just call her when he's misbehaving. Katie nods. But then she goes about the business of being a highly ambivalent big sister.

Allison knows something is amiss. Yes, it's possible, at least at times, that Katie believes she is being grown-up and "helping" Johnny get places and do things. But Allison also suspects that her behavior is fueled by jealousy and that her excessively physical ways of interacting with Johnny are actually expressions of her resentment over the great deal of Allison's attention he demands.

Of course, Katie could be a big help to her mother if she would entertain Johnny while Allison is making dinner or walk next to him in the grocery store. But those are the times Katie seems unaware she even has a little brother. It's big sister time, it seems, only if she can throw her (and his) weight around.

Allison would really like Katie to enjoy being an older sister. There is so much for her to do that could make her feel older, wiser, and proud. Also, Allison needs to be sure that Johnny does not sustain any injuries!

★ FIRST, TALKING ABOUT IT ★

Allison realizes that in the past she has often spoken to Katie about how wonderful it is to have a younger sibling. She can teach him things! Help him! Have fun playing with him when he gets older! But now Allison decides to take a different tack.

She decides to commiserate.

"Katie," she begins. "I think there are good parts and bad parts to having a younger brother. We sure have discussed all the fun parts, but I've been thinking, it must be hard when I have to spend a lot of time watching him, and giving him baths, and putting him to bed. It takes a lot of time."

Katie doesn't say anything for a minute. Then she comments quietly, "Well, he does cry a lot." She looks at Allison with a poignant expression. It seems to say, "I'm a little tired of him. Is that OK?"

"He does," Allison agrees. "I don't like hearing his crying either." She pauses. "And besides, I miss you. I want to spend more time with you. Private time," she says warmly.

Katie lights up. "Oh! What should we do?"

"We'll talk about it," Allison answers. "But in order for us to spend time together, I am going to need some help from you with Johnny. I could get things done faster, like making dinner and getting groceries."

"I help," Katie says looking at her mom a tad defensively.

Allison wants to be careful here because Katie is likely largely unaware that the way she treats Johnny is expressing something other than concern. "I do appreciate that you do lots of things with Johnny, but when you do things like carrying him around, I get worried for both of you. You could drop him by accident, or you could trip and hurt yourself. It would be better if you played with him on the floor."

Katie shrugs. "I like playing with him my way."

Allison has to smile at that. "Yes, I'm sure you do," she says gently. "But I'm going to have to ask that you help me by playing with him in some different ways. Because if you do, I have a great idea to make sure we get to do some special activities together!"

Katie is immediately drawn in when Allison offers as a reward a special outing for just her and Katie to the ice skating rink. She's been begging for lessons lately, and Allison suggests that if she can be helpful for one week, the two of them can go skating together. If she manages it a second week, she earns herself a "professional" lesson, and then the two of them will skate for the rest of the session.

"OK!" Katie sings out. "What should I do?"

★ THE REWARD PLAN ★

Allison has chosen the Pockets for Points chart (see the Pull-Out section at the back of the book) to keep track of Katie's behaviors, because she thinks the hands-on format will appeal to her. Also, given that some of Katie's interactions with Johnny could cause physical injury, she feels she must include a penalty for misbehavior, which the Pockets for Points chart can easily accommodate.

Allison shows Katie what she has created. She's cut out the pieces for the Pockets for Points chart and taped the Points Won! and Points Lost pockets onto the chart. She then asks Katie to help her cut out the Sun and Cloud Point Slips to use with the chart. She helps Katie color the clouds gray and the suns all sorts of bright colors. (An illustration of this chart in use can be found on p. 125 in Part 3.)

Allison explains to Katie that she can earn a Sun Point if
- She tells her mom when Johnny is getting into trouble.
- She shows books to Johnny when Allison is making dinner.
- She teaches Johnny a new behavior.
- She does something to make Johnny happy.

Katie will get a Cloud Point if
- She picks up and carries Johnny.
- She tosses Johnny onto the bed without Allison being there.
- She pulls Johnny down from a chair or stool.

Allison reviews the behaviors with Katie, role-playing some of them to help Katie remember what she can do to earn Sun Points and to avoid Cloud Points. Allison explains to Katie that her goal will be to earn at least 5 Sun Points each day, and to avoid receiving more than 2 Cloud Points. To make the goal very clear and concrete for Katie, Allison takes the Pockets for Points chart and says "Let's pretend you just did something nice to Johnny. Then you would get to put a Sun Point in this pocket. And if you fill up this pocket with 5, 6, or even more Sun Points, you'll be doing great!" Katie smiles and places several Sun Points in the Points Won! pocket.

"But," continues Allison, "you're going to have to be careful not to get too many Cloud Points. If you get more than 2 Cloud Points in one day, you're not going to be able to get a star for that day, even if you've gotten 5 Sun Points. And you need to get 7 stars for us to be able to go skating together. When you earn a star, I'll put it on this piece of paper," Allison says, showing Katie the Daily Checklist (see p. 123 for an illustration of this chart). "If you miss getting a star one day, you'll have to try extra hard the next day." (Allison has decided not to require Katie to reach the point goal for 7 days straight; she wouldn't want Katie to fail after being successful for a number of days.)

To begin, Allison places all the points in the Point Keeper pocket at the bottom of the chart. Each time Katie does something helpful, Allison inserts a Sun Point in the Points Won! pocket. If she slips, a Cloud Point goes into the Points Lost pocket. At the end of each day, Allison returns all the points to the Point Keeper pocket, and if Katie has been successful in meeting the point goal that day, Allison puts a star on the Daily Checklist.

Allison hangs the chart up on the refrigerator high enough so Johnny can't reach it, but it is low enough for Katie on her tiptoes to insert her points. Anticipating that Johnny might feel left out, Allison has photocopied the chart pages and given him his own Pockets for Points chart, which he can play with as he chooses. Johnny imitates Katie, and for a brief time whenever he offers Katie a toy, he asks for a point. Allison praises him and gives him a point on his chart. Johnny does not understand the connection between the points and the ice skating outing, and he asks for no larger reward.

★ WHAT HAPPENS ★

Katie's excitement about the Reward Plan translates into a much more peaceful home. To keep the tone of the program positive, Allison tries to help Katie avoid losing too many points (for example, when she's clearly in an aggressive mood, by suggesting that she play in her room for a while).

After the first week, Katie is rarely treating Johnny roughly, and Allison compliments her gener-

ously. Then, Allison tells Katie that the next week she'll have to earn at least 7 Sun Points and no more than 1 Cloud Point to get a star for that day. Katie accepts this more challenging goal, and 8 days later she has earned her skating lesson.

The obvious rewards are that Allison and Katie get some wonderful private time together, and Katie gets the lesson she has yearned for. But perhaps more important, Katie gives herself a chance to feel Johnny's admiration when she stops to teach him something. (He's learning his colors because of her!) In fact, a shopper at the local grocery store, who was listening to Katie say, "See Johnny? The red cookie box?" commented "What a good sister you are!"

Katie, Allison could tell, felt like the sun, the moon, and the stars!

NO BORROWING WITHOUT ASKING

Ten-year-old Melissa and 9-year-old Karen haven't mastered the art of sharing. Somehow, "borrowing" has been defined as taking without asking with the intent of giving back but with little regard to when and in what shape. (This happened with the perfect-colored T-shirt to go with a skirt that got stained.) Losing or breaking something borrowed brings on a case of "amnesia," whereby the person doing the taking forgets she did so. (This often occurs with plastic bracelets, beads, or barrettes.) The only time "May I borrow" leaves the lips of either girl is when she wants something she can't slip away without being noticed. Then, if the answer is no, sometimes she borrows it anyway, with the reason, "She was just being mean, and I needed it and she didn't." (This happened when one daughter went to a party and the other did not.)

Their mother Stephanie can see that each girl seems to feel the other has more or better. Also, it is apparent that each believes the other ought to be sharing and when she doesn't is simply being mean.

Most important, Stephanie is also seeing that Melissa and Karen are failing to respect the needs and desires of the other and contributing to an atmosphere of distrust and jealousy. Stephanie knows they are close enough in age so that in many ways they could be an important source of support for each other. She wants to help them begin taking steps to get there . . . before the struggle between them becomes too ingrained to change any time soon or, worse, ever.

★First, Talking About It★

Stephanie sits the girls down on Saturday morning when neither daughter is fuming over a "borrowed" item. "Girls," she begins, "This arguing over who can use who's stuff, and who borrows what, and who can't touch this or that has to stop."

"She's always taking my things!" both girls cry out almost in unison.

"I know," Stephanie says soothingly. "But there are lots of good parts to having a sister who wears the same size clothes. You both like to borrow, but sometimes it's hard to have your own things borrowed, particularly if you don't expect it."

The girls quiet down. Stephanie has managed to get them to think positively, and they are now more in a mood to work together.

Stephanie continues. "I have a plan to help you work on sharing in a way I think you are both going to feel comfortable with. It will help you identify what's off limits, what's not, and what the rules are for asking to borrow. It'll be clear. And if you work at it, you'll have a chance to each earn one of those beaded shirts you've been wanting." (Beaded shirts are currently a "must-have" item!)

★The Reward Plan★

Stephanie gives each girl a Keeping Track chart (for a blank one, see the Pull-Out section at the back of the book) and labels the first column "Asking Permission," the second "Agreeing to Share," and the third "Explain Why Not Sharing." She says they are going to keep track of these behaviors for 3 weeks. She assures them that each girl has a right to sometimes say no to a request, but they have to record the reason. This is a way of keeping track so if there's conflict later, Stephanie can evaluate the reasons and possibly help work out a compromise.

Stephanie then asks Karen and Melissa to discuss and agree on what would be good reasons to say no to a request to borrow a piece of clothing or other item. They agree on the following:

- It's new, and its owner has worn it only one or two times.
- The owner fears that the borrower is going to get it dirty because she'll be at a picnic or other messy place.
- One of them wants to wear her own article of clothing, hair item,

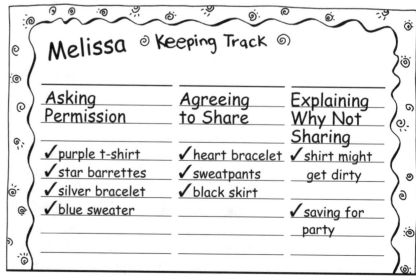

Keeping Track Chart

or jewelry.

- The item is just very special to the owner. The three decide that this can only apply to a few agreed-on items, whereupon a small argument ensues as to which ones. Eventually, each girl settles on five items. Neither girl can ask for these things.

Finally Stephanie explains to the girls how they will keep track of successful sharing:

1. Each time a girl asks permission to borrow an item, she gets a check mark in column 1 on her chart and records the item.
2. Each time a girl agrees to share, she gets a check mark and lists the item in column 2.
3. Each time a girl explains a reason for not sharing, she gets a check mark in column 3, plus she records her reason for saying no.

Stephanie and her daughters agree that after 3 weeks, Melissa and Karen will earn the beaded shirts if each has asked permission at least 15 times and each has agreed to share at least 10 times.

If one girl has accumulated enough points and the other hasn't, then Stephanie will wait until the other one has achieved her quota before purchasing the shirts. (At that point, Stephanie expects a flurry of asking and agreeing, so that the shirt purchase will not be delayed for long!)

★ WHAT HAPPENS ★

The girls move into this plan easily and spend a great deal of time considering catalogs. The Keeping Track charts quickly fill up with check marks, and the squabbling between sisters is much reduced. By the time they earn their shirts, they actually consult with each other in the store about which colors they should buy so that each of them can use the other's with equal enthusiasm.

The girls are operating like a team! It's invisible to them, but clear to their delighted mother.

"I'll Do It Later!"

DOING THE CHORES

No child enjoys chores. They aren't fun, and they require self-discipline. They are a *responsibility*. Being asked to make beds, put dishes in a dishwasher, fold the laundry, set the table, sweep up after dinner, or simply drag out the trash containers can seem to children like nothing more than big-time unwanted obligations. And why not?

After all, next door, Bobby doesn't have to do these things. Besides, isn't school exhausting enough? And what about playtime? After school activities? Anyway, "I'm just a kid!"

Getting children to do their chores, for most parents, can be a very trying endeavor. You probably grew up with a set of chores you were expected to complete. Almost definitely, your parents had plenty of chores when they were young, and when you were a child they may have listed them for you ad infinitum. You might have thought to yourself as an adolescent, "When I have kids, I'm not making them do a thing."

And so here you are. The truth is, you really don't want to tax your kids unduly. You do see they have busy days. On the other hand, you've probably also learned that your parents and their parents had a point. There is something character building about contributing to the running of one's home. It underlines the idea that you are a family and that you need each other in emotional and practical ways. Also, even a modest amount of help from a child with two working parents or a single parent can make a big difference.

So are rewards appropriate here? Shouldn't children just, well, do the job and that's that? Many parents would argue for this. But the problem is, times have changed. Your children aren't growing up in a society where children have to "work," and the many families they visit likely have a variety of expectations, with some having few or no expectations of children helping. This environment gives children room to take stands, argue, or rebel. There is no strict norm.

Certainly, promising extravagant rewards would completely undermine the purpose and lesson behind chores. But modest rewards, together with discussions that explore how chores are a way of caring for one's family, are reasonable. Your Reward Plan can involve the entire family, which is a nice idea considering chores are something that is supposed to be for the common good, or it can focus on a pair of siblings or just one individual child.

If you are trying to involve the entire family in a concrete chore schedule, an incentive might be a fun outing together. You can use the excursion to emphasize that when everyone contributes to the running of the home, there is more time for enjoyable group activities. The real heart of doing chores is the fact that it is an expression of your family's unity—a unity that is in itself a gift. In doing a chore, you are displaying true responsibility and respect for each other.

If you are devising a Reward Plan for chores for an individual child or a pair of children, it is reasonable to tie a weekly allowance to their performance. Linking chores to an allowance is a way of saying, "I know an allowance will make your life more comfortable, but you must work as a unit with us and make our lives more comfortable as well." You will be trading reasonable expectations. Your children expect an allowance, and you expect some help.

This section provides an in-depth sample Reward Plan for
• a family with children ages 10 and 7 in which Mom, Dad, and children all participate in the plan,
plus briefer plans for
• a 5-year-old girl who doesn't pick up her toys and
• a 9-year-old boy who resists doing chores.

ALL WORKING TOGETHER

Ten-year-old Tasha and 7-year-old Dante cannot seem to complete their chores in a timely, efficient, and responsible manner. They've always done their chores in a half-hearted fashion, causing their mother, Robin, to give frequent reminders and occasional scoldings. Now, because Robin has recently increased her work hours, she has less patience for their dawdling. Lately she feels as if she's taken on an extra new part-time job: the family nag.

Robin has asked the children to work together in setting and then clearing the dinner table. Later, Tasha is to help with loading the dishwasher. Typically, the children end up accusing each other of not doing their fair share, and often both walk away with their jobs only partially done.

Robin also has asked each of them to do a chore on the weekend. Tasha is supposed to help sort and fold the laundry on Saturday morning, and Dante is to put his clothes away in his drawers. But Tasha rarely does her laundry duty on Saturday morning because she is very eager to go outside and play with friends. Most of the laundry ends up in front of the laundry closet only partially sorted. Dante drags his feet putting his clothes away, usually toting only half the pile into his room, and then shoving what he can into whichever drawer is easiest for him to reach. The rest sits on the floor and serves as a nice pillow for the family cat to snooze on.

And it's not just the children Robin's been nagging. Now that she's working more hours, she would like more help at home from her husband, Rod. If he would help prepare dinner or clean the pots and pans, Robin would be able to spend more time helping the children with homework.

★ First, Talking About It ★

Robin begins by talking to Rod to see whether he will agree to trying a Reward Plan. She tells him that she's sorry she's been losing her temper with him for not helping out more. She realizes he works hard at his job, she says, but she is finding the adjustment to increased work hours more difficult than she anticipated. Rod appreciates the apology and tells her he's often so tired in the evening that it's tough for him to get used to getting out of his chair and helping her in the kitchen. But he sees that she's tired, too.

Rod says that he, like Robin, has been frustrated by Tasha's and Dante's whining and resistance to doing chores. However, he's a bit skeptical about a Reward Plan. Robin is not surprised by his skepticism. In fact, she's already thought of a way to make the plan more appealing to him. Everyone in the family will have to work at earning points, and *her* job will be to nag less! Rod chuckles and says, "Now, that's not a bad idea!" He signs on to the plan.

Rod has always wanted the family to start a tradition in which the entire family goes out to Renzo's, the neighborhood Italian restaurant, on Sunday evenings. The children very much enjoy it there (in particular, they like the spumoni!). In the past, Robin had nixed the idea because she felt compelled to watch the budget. But things are a little more relaxed now. Robin decides with Rod that the family dinner out would be a great reward for everyone.

On Sunday evening, Robin and Rod sit down with the children and open a discussion about chores. To keep the conversation positive, they decide to focus on the desirability of having a happier family life rather than zeroing in on the children's lack of responsibility. "I wish we had more time to do some fun things together," Robin begins. "It seems like so many times when we're together, I'm just getting after you about doing your chores."

Tasha and Dante are quiet. They're not sure where this discussion is heading.

Rod decides to jump in and introduce the Reward Plan. "Your mother and I have been thinking about how we can all be happier getting the work done that's needed to keep this family going. We thought we could set up a chart showing our jobs and keep track of how everyone's doing. And if we all do our work each week, we could go out together on Sunday evenings to Renzo's, to sort of celebrate."

Tasha's face brightens. "Can I get spumoni?" she asks.

"Sure," her father says. "As long as I can get some, too!"

"But I do think everyone is going to have to put a little more effort into doing things well," Robin cautions. She pauses. "What do you think I'm going to work on?"

The children look at Robin curiously.

"I'm going to work on stopping yelling at everyone!" she announces.

Tasha and Dante look at each other and smile. Rod smiles, too. And Robin smiles to herself. Little do they know—she may have the easiest and most rewarding job of all!

★ THE REWARD PLAN ★

Robin explains to the children that everyone will get check marks when they do their jobs. If everyone tries hard all week, they'll go out to Renzo's Sunday evening. Rather than specifying the exact number of check marks that have to be accumulated, Robin emphasizes that the reward will be based on everyone trying hard. She is counting on the likelihood that no one will want to seem the shirker.

She brings out a piece of paper and suggests that the family think about what everyone's goals will be. Robin has jotted down the following preliminary list:

Mom: asks people to help nicely.
Dad: helps with dinner preparation or cleanup.
Tasha: helps Dante set the table and clear away dishes, loads dishwasher, and sorts and folds laundry.
Dante: helps Tasha set the table and clear away dishes, and puts away his clean clothes.

"So, does everyone know what they have to do?" Robin asks.

Rod looks at the list and chuckles. "Looks like the kids are doing more than we are!" Robin raises her eyebrows. "It does, indeed!" she says, playing along with her husband.

Rod continues, "Let's see, is there anything else we do?" He turns to the children and suggests they help him make a list of the chores their mother does.

The children are quiet for a moment. Then Dante says, "You cook, Mom!" Robin responds with a smile. "Well, I guess I do." Never one to be left behind, Tasha quickly comes up with a list of Robin's responsibilities. "Dante, Mom does the laundry, shopping, cleaning, makes our lunches, pays the bills . . ." "Whoa!" Rod protests. "I can't write that quickly!" Robin helps him out by suggesting that he might just summarize her chores as "keeps the house running." Tasha and Dante nod, obviously impressed by the number of chores Robin's been doing without their having given it much thought.

Then it's time to summarize Dad's chores. After the children have brainstormed and come up with a long list that Robin summarizes as "keeps everything else running," she turns to the children. She begins by saying that she has thought about their chores and decided that it might be better if they took turns with setting and clearing the table, rather than working together on both parts. On one day, Dante will set and Tasha will clear, and the following day they'll change jobs. Despite the emphasis on family teamwork, Robin's decided that sharing the tasks of table setting and clearing leaves too much room for her rivalrous children to feel that the other one isn't pulling his or her weight.

"Now, do you kids know what you've got to do?" Robin asks.

Tasha looks thoughtful, a slight frown on her face. "Well, I know we don't have to do as much as you and Dad. But you're grown-ups—you're supposed to do those things," Tasha says tentatively. Then she turns her attention to her own list of chores. "It's good that Dante and I will take turns with setting and clearing the table. But . . ." Tasha pauses.

Robin suspects what's coming. However, even though she'd love to hear that everyone is eager to work as a team member, she figures it's better if Tasha expresses any reservations now about the chore assignments.

"What is it, Tasha?" she says encouragingly. Tasha continues, a bit timidly, "Well, it's never seemed fair that Dante doesn't have as many chores as I do. I have to load the dishwasher, and I have more laundry to take care of."

Rod frowns. Robin can see he's not pleased by Tasha's attitude. Robin jumps in and attempts to address Tasha's feelings that things aren't fair. "Tasha, your brother really can't load the dishwasher. He's not tall enough to rinse the dishes. Anyway, when you were his age, you only had to clear the table."

Dante pipes up. "It's OK. I'll help put the forks and stuff in the dishwasher. I'm tall enough for that!"

"That's great, Dante," Robin responds, delighted that he has bought into the idea of the family working as a team. "I guess we should all help each other when we can. And if I slip, someone ought to tell me if I sound like I'm nagging, OK?"

"Hey, is anyone going to help me?" Rod asks.

"I'll dry the pots," Robin laughs, "But maybe I can do something more. How about if I ask how your

Our Family Chore Chart

Let's Go to Renzo's!

	MON	TUES	WED	THURS	FRI	SAT	SUN		
Mom keeps house running / asks for help nicely / asks Dad how day was	✓ ✓ ✓	✓ ✓ ✓	✓ ✓ ✓	▭ ▭ ▭	▭ ▭ ▭	▭ ▭ ▭	FREE DAY		
Dad keeps everything running / helps with dinner	✓ ✓	✓ ✓	✓ ✓	▭ ▭	▭ ▭	▭ ▭	OUT TO DINNER!		
Tasha sets table / clears table / laundry	✓	✓	✓	▭	▭	▭ ▭	↓		
Dante sets table / clears table / laundry	✓	✓	✓	▭	▭	▭			

Design-Your-Own Chart

Design-Your-Own Chart

day went?"

"Wouldn't mind that," Rod nods.

Having gotten an agreement, Robin fills out a Design-Your-Own chart (for a blank one, see the Pull-Out section at the back of the book). She lists each family member's name in the left hand column in a separate space, then writes out that person's chores. To help Tasha and Dante remember whose evening it is to set or clear the table, Robin adds small boxes for check marks underneath the days of the week to indicate when a chore needs to be done.

★ WHAT HAPPENS ★

That evening's cleanup period is remarkably cooperative and pleasant. Robin suggests turning on some music to help get the chores done, and she hears Tasha humming along. Dante, very eager to be a "big kid," does indeed load the silverware into the washer. During the next few days, the family works together harmoniously. Then, on Friday, both Robin and Rod come home unusually tired. Rod slumps in his chair, and Robin faces the task of making dinner alone. She begins to grumble.

"Mom," Tasha whispers. "You're nagging Daddy."

Robin sighs. Yes, she's nagging. But she wishes her husband could see how tired she is. Then she remembers her lines. "How was your day?"

"A nightmare," Rod replies. "Constant phone calls . . . worst day in months."

"I'm sorry," Robin says softly. "Mine was pretty hard, too."

Rod, thankfully, follows Robin to the kitchen. "Sorry. What can I help with?"

"Would you mind cutting up the beans?" she asks.

They've salvaged the evening. Weekend comes, and the children manage the laundry surprisingly quickly and efficiently. Sunday evening, they are all off to the Italian restaurant.

After the first week's success, Robin makes a new chart and continues the plan another week. Periodically, one or another family member slips into old patterns, but with just a little prodding the chore gets done—especially, Robin notices, when the person is given just a little help or moral support. Whenever this happens, she says something like, "Gee, it sure is easier to do what you're supposed to do when someone says, 'I'll give you a hand!'" They go for spumoni again on Sunday.

After a month, Robin can see that the weekly dinner trip has become a family ritual, and cooperation has become more the norm than dawdling and quarreling. She stops making charts, and chores go smoothly for several months. Then some of the old habits begin to creep back in. Dante and Tasha procrastinate, Rod slumps in his chair, and Robin begins to nag. One evening she actually dissolves into tears. Then, bless his heart, it's Dante who pipes up and announces at dinner, "We need a new chart!"

★ THE INVISIBLE REWARDS ★

In addition to learning what the spirit of cooperation is all about, Tasha and Dante have been presented with a number of important lessons. Robin's and Rod's willingness to participate in the plan has underlined that chores are a family matter. And Robin's willingness to admit that her own behavior could stand improvement has also conveyed to them that the challenge to improve one's behavior is a lifelong task and nothing to be ashamed of.

Finally, doing chores together is one of those moments when the family gets to feel like a team. The authority issue melts into the background while everyone does something equally important.

One more thing. During the duration of the plan, and for a good while thereafter, Robin's delighted that the family no longer needs a nag.

★ ALSO WORKS FOR . . . ★

A chart that includes all members of the family (or even just two children) can be a constant reminder that everyone is in this together. It helps keep track of when everyone has to do their responsibilities. This kind of chart can be used for activities such as

- keeping track of belongings,
- dog walking,
- cleaning the cat litter, and
- returning library books.

REMEMBERING TO PICK UP

Five-year-old Christy has never been very good about picking up her toys after playing with them in the family room. Elaine always had a relaxed attitude about this and would only periodically remind Christy to put them away. However, Elaine's mother Dorothy has just moved into their home for a while, and Elaine worries that her mother might trip and fall should a toy be left on the floor. Dorothy's recently been quite sick, and Elaine is concerned that she is unsteady on her feet. Since her grandmother's arrival, Christy has picked up toys when Elaine reminds her, but she rarely remembers on her own.

Elaine is now feeling the stress of caring for her weakened mother and recognizes that she has been speaking more and more sharply to Christy about toys left on the floor. Christy has twice burst out crying after Elaine has reprimanded her. Christy enjoys her grandmother's company and, because she is a very kind child, also enjoys helping her. But Christy's finding it hard to learn the habit of picking up after playing. Elaine recognizes that this is a hard habit for a 5-year-old to master. She also can see that Christy occasionally looks a bit upset when she sees that her grandmother, who only last year was quite vigorous, seems so slow and worn out.

★ FIRST, TALKING ABOUT IT ★

Early one morning when the family room is neatened up, Elaine sits down beside Christy and asks her how it feels to have Grandma living with them for a while. Christy immediately looks a little sad.

"Good," Christy says, "and bad." She tells Elaine that she loves her grandmother but that when she wobbles a little, it scares her. Elaine assures her that her grandmother will be getting better as soon as the doctors get her medication straight and that Elaine knows it's hard for Christy. Then she segues into keeping the family room neat. "I'm sorry I get so upset with you, honey, when you don't put away your toys. I just don't want Grandma to trip and fall."

Christy nods. She's a perceptive and understanding child.

★ THE REWARD PLAN ★

Then Elaine tells her that she has a fun plan to help her remember to pick up her toys. She shows her the Playhouse chart (see the Pull-Out section) and tells her that she can earn a sticker to place on the chart whenever she remembers to clean up when she's through playing. Elaine's bought her an assortment of stickers including food and household items and toys, plus some flowers and birds for the outside. Jokingly, Elaine tells her that this is her house, and she can put things anywhere she wants. Toys can even be left on the floor! (An example of this chart with stickers affixed can be found on p. 124 in Part 3.)

★ WHAT HAPPENS ★

Elaine tapes the chart up on the wall in the family room. Christy is delighted and promptly pulls out her dolls, briefly plays with them, then puts them away and asks for her first sticker. Elaine compliments her daughter and lets her choose one. She starts with the kitten, and Elaine helps her stick it in place.

All morning, Christy pulls out toys, plays with them a short while, then puts them away. Recognizing that this burst of enthusiasm won't last long, Elaine continues to praise her efforts and offer stickers. She earns five that morning. After the first week, the chart is getting very congested (Elaine had to go out and buy a couple more packages of stickers), and Christy is still cleaning up fairly consistently. But she is starting to lose interest in the chart, and every once in a while she forgets to pick up her toys. Elaine gently reminds her, and sheepishly she cleans up. Elaine doesn't want her to feel so guilty. She reassures Christy that she knows she is trying very hard. But Elaine realizes that they may need a new plan to keep Christy focused on the need to pick up.

Dorothy has noticed how well Christy has been doing and has enjoyed her interest in the Playhouse chart. She remembers that Elaine's old dollhouse is packed in a box in the attic of her own home. Dorothy takes Elaine aside and proposes that she give it to Christy. Elaine thinks quickly and suggests that her old dollhouse would provide a great new reward. "How about we have Christy earn the furniture to the dollhouse?" she suggests to her mother.

Together, Elaine and Dorothy tell Christy that every day she doesn't forget to pick up her toys, she will earn one piece of furniture. They unpack the dollhouse and place it on a table in the family room—a very visible reminder. Christy is delighted with the dollhouse and walks around the first day saying, over and over, "Remember to pick up! Remember to pick up!"

The high point comes a week later, when Dorothy is feeling well enough to sit down on the floor next to Christy, peer into the house, and discuss interior decorating. Elaine smiles. Not only is the family room neater and safer for her mother, but the Reward Plan has actually involved all three of them, giving Christy a chance to once more experience Dorothy's joyous spirit.

LEARNING TO TAKE RESPONSIBILITY

Paul is now 9 years old and is currently responsible only for putting the newspapers into paper bags once a week for recycling. His father, Joe, feels that Paul should be doing more to contribute to the household, but it's a difficult road. Paul is an only child, and Joe realizes that he's been pretty lax about asking Paul to contribute around the house. Joe is starting to worry that Paul will not develop a sense of responsibility or, if he does, certainly not toward the family. Joe and his wife Carol have talked to Paul about additional chores, suggesting he be responsible for watering the indoor plants or putting the dishes in the dishwasher after dinner.

But Paul is resistant—and he's got a good argument. Joe's sister, who lives nearby, has indulged her own 9-year-old daughter, and Paul is well aware that she does nothing around the house. "Tara doesn't do anything. Why do I have to?" Paul regularly insists. Joe always hesitates. He can't put his thoughts into words. "Because you need to develop a sense of responsibility" sounds so unconvincing to him. So trite. He wonders whether it's worth the struggle.

But one day, after Paul glares at Joe for suggesting that he bring the recycling containers out to the curb, he decides it is.

★ FIRST, TALKING ABOUT IT ★

Joe and Carol sit down with Paul and begin a discussion about chores. Actually, it's more like a debate. Paul challenges them immediately. "Tara doesn't do any. You just want me to do it to prove something. You don't really need me to help. You just want me to work because you think I won't get spoiled that way." Joe is aghast at Paul's heated resistance to assuming some responsibility. But he also blames himself for not having introduced chores at a younger age.

Paul is not entirely wrong about Joe's reasoning. But he's only 9, and he doesn't have much understanding about the long-term consequences of being "spoiled." Rather than getting into an argument, Joe calmly responds, "Is that why you think we want you to have some chores?" Paul looks a bit surprised and then answers, "Yeah. You probably read in a book somewhere that kids should have them."

"Yes, we have, but we also have our own ideas . . . and here they are," Carol states firmly. "I think that lots of things you do when you're young will help you do more important things when you get older. I remember last year, when your third-grade teacher said she wanted to give you homework so you'd get used to it. She didn't want it to be hard for you when you started getting more work in fourth grade."

"That's different," Paul mutters quietly.

Joe continues the discussion. "But another thing we haven't been giving you experience with is in handling money. We've bought you the things that you need. But we've never given you an allowance so that you could have practice keeping track of your own money."

Paul becomes more attentive. "Can I get an allowance?" Joe can see the eagerness on his face. How in the world, Joe bets he's thinking, did this conversation go from doing chores to getting money?

"Yes. It would be quite reasonable for you to receive an allowance if you start doing some chores. I'm offering an allowance because you are taking on responsibilities and so are old enough to begin to budget yourself as well."

★ THE REWARD PLAN ★

Joe has gotten Paul's interest and pushes on with negotiations. "I've been thinking that along with taking care of the newspapers, you might start with setting the table before dinner and then helping to clear everyone's dishes off the table after dinner is finished."

Joe specifies that if Paul performs these tasks five times each week, he will get a $3 weekly allowance. They will put check marks on the kitchen calendar when the jobs are done. To further engage Paul's interest, Joe suggests that the two of them write up a contract. Joe comments, "This is what may happen when you're older and get a job. You'll sign a contract that says the work you'll do and what salary you'll receive." Joe takes out a piece of lined notebook paper, places the date at the top, and jots down their agreement. He then signs his name and gives it to Paul for him to sign as well.

Paul hesitates before he signs it. "What's this about bringing the newspapers out to the corner? I always have to rush out of the house because I'm going to be late for school."

"Well, I think you're smart enough to be able to plan your time a little more carefully," Joe responds, offering a compliment rather than chiding Paul for his poor planning. "But good for you for reading the fine print!"

"What does that mean?" Paul asks.

"It means you should never sign a contract without reading every word carefully. Otherwise, you could agree to do something that isn't fair or right. No one's ever going to be able to put anything over on you!"

Paul quickly signs, clearly inflated by his contract prowess. Joe adds his signature and then files the contract with his business papers.

★ WHAT HAPPENS ★

Paul needs an occasional reminder to set the table before dinner, and he is a bit slower in getting the chores done than his father would like. But he does live up to his side of the deal, and he doesn't dally in asking for his allowance at the end of the week!

Joe feels proud that he's found a way to help build a sense of responsibility in his son and has introduced the notion of a budget at the same time.

It's rewarding to know you are preparing your child to deal with real life.

"I Hardly Have Any!"

REDUCING HOMEWORK BLUES

S omewhere in the world, there exist children who tackle their homework independently, efficiently, effectively, and with enthusiasm. If you're reading this section, however, you're probably not the lucky parent of one of these self-motivated beings! So often, I listen to parents report spending their evenings reminding, chiding, nagging, threatening, bribing, and on occasion virtually doing their children's homework for them.

This evening routine can become tragically ritualized and can come close to ruining much of the precious time the whole family has together. Fortunately, there are plenty of things you can do to put an end to the homework nightmare. But first, you have to take a cool, calm look at the particulars. Much of what you do will depend on how and why your child is having problems with homework.

Some children dawdle, spending hours working their way through homework assignments in between stringing beads, daydreaming, and trying on a new pair of jeans. Others procrastinate endlessly about even starting their work. "The dog needs to be walked." "As *soon* as I finish this painting." "I'm hungry!"

Then there are those children who rush through, or rather over, assignments as if they're bulldozers in a race for time. They barrel through, barely looking at what they're producing. It's all just a vast wasteland of numbers and words to them. Sure, the math page is done, but careless errors are everywhere, and if this is brought to their attention, they might reply, "The teacher says we're allowed to make mistakes!" And let's not forget those kids who are somewhat insecure, who think they can't do it without you, and who, the moment you walk away, do the same. It's true they may need some help here and there, but without you they can't (or believe they can't) think.

Finally, there's the problem of lost or misplaced workbooks, assignment pads that don't make it home, and completed homework that doesn't make it back to school. For some children, learning to be organized is at least half the battle.

So what do you do besides argue, threaten, stand there until there's some level of compliance, or take away every privilege available to your child?

First, you want to be sure your child does not have a learning problem that the school hasn't discovered. Many children with learning disabilities would prefer to look lazy, defiant, or disorganized than to show they can't do the work. They don't want others to believe what they secretly think—that they are having trouble because they are stupid.

Many parents worry that promising children rewards for academic work will discourage them from discovering a genuine interest in school subjects. Reward Plans may feel fine to parents who are trying to get teeth brushed and put a stop to hitting, but when it comes to learning, somehow they fear it will devalue education. But here's a fact you should know: Studies have shown that rewards, when designed well, can move children to higher levels of mastery. These studies show that if you reward high-quality work, children will improve the quality of work they produce. And that sets the stage for continuing academic success.

How does one go from rewards for doing schoolwork to motivation that comes from within? First, through Reward Plans, children can be encouraged to work on building-block skills that will give them the foundation they need for future learning. Feeling successful early on will make children more eager, and

more ready, to face academic challenges in later grades. Second, having experienced the broad range of invisible rewards that accompany work well done, children most often begin to understand what a little work can do for a person. The obvious approval of the teacher's "Good job!" as she hands back the paper in front of others feels like an Academy Award. The bright red "100%" feels great. The admiration of peers is an added boon. And perhaps the most important bonus comes when your child suddenly realizes that he knows something . . . and that it can be applied to what he learns next, and that suddenly everything is getting easier. These are all rewards your child simply cannot easily anticipate while she is busy brushing the cat as you dangle the geography page in front of her nose!

Once your child has these experiences, he will start to value learning. Of course, you may still have a spotty time of it. But things will undoubtedly improve if you focus on his particular problem and develop the most effective Reward Plan for him.

If homework is regularly not completed, then the reward will have to hinge on your child stepping up to the plate and getting it all done. If the quality of the homework is the problem, then you will have to delineate for your child exactly what constitutes acceptable work and reward improved quality. If procrastination is the devil in the closet, then the two of you will have to agree on what it means to get homework done on time and figure out a way to help your child avoid distractions. Then you can offer the reward once your child makes a real effort to just sit down and do the job. And of course, if your child fears she cannot do it herself, you might need to explore whether she is indeed having a problem at school and needs testing, or whether you simply have to wean her off your presence.

Parents sometimes ask me about offering a reward or money for each A at the end of a marking period. I actually don't think much of this idea. I believe it's much more important to concern yourself with the process of achieving good grades than with the good grades themselves. Those often come naturally once the homework is done. Besides, what if you have a child who, no matter how hard he tries, cannot make top grades? Withholding a reward that is beyond his ability to attain can feel like punishment. Solid B and C students with good work habits (and perhaps with strengths in areas outside the classroom) have the potential to be very successful in life and shouldn't be made to feel inadequate in any way.

Finally, let me just address one problem that most every parent and child faces at one time or another: Teachers who give endless or boring assignments are a fixture in the field of education. Sometimes you can suggest, in the most tactful of ways, that slight modifications be made. "Gee, Mr. Cabot, every week you ask the kids to take 10 words and write a sentence using each. Would you mind if Jimmy wrote them into a funny story? I think he'd like to do that." Mr. Cabot may nod and say all right, or he may frown and then just continue along his merry soporific way. If it's the latter case, you will simply have to turn this into a life lesson for your child. Don't deny his reality, but don't put down Mr. Cabot either. Especially if this is a younger child, your words are bound to be repeated in the wrong place. You might tell your child, "I understand that you don't like the homework assignments. But Mr. Cabot thinks this is a good way to teach you, and we're just going to have to go along with it."

"It's *soooo* boring" may be a legitimate complaint that deserves some sympathy, but it isn't a legitimate excuse for not doing homework.

TARGETING PROCRASTINATION

Ten-year-old Adam has always been a stubborn child, but he has a creative mind and can easily be drawn into novel challenges. Unfortunately, his fifth-grade curriculum, as his teacher is handling it, is largely drill work. Most of Adam's creativity is being stifled, and so is his desire to please.

The year began with him sitting at his desk every evening for a decent amount of time (perhaps an hour altogether), but there were always those forays. Sometimes he'd wander over to see what his younger sister was watching on television. Other times, he seemed to feel compelled to neaten his shelves. His father, Randy, would admonish him, and he'd return to his desk, taking pencil in hand. The only problem was, every time he poked his head into Adam's room, that pencil was being twirled. "Are you getting your homework done?" Randy would ask, trying hard not to sound accusatory. "Yes," Adam would call out, the annoyance obvious in his voice. Randy would shrug, hoping it was so.

But then the first note comes home from school indicating that Adam is not getting his work done. In fact, rarely is even a single assignment being fully completed! Randy asks Adam what is going on, and he tells him in no uncertain terms: "It's stupid." On Randy's insistence, he shows him his assignments, and he can certainly see that the math, vocabulary, and spelling assignments are numbingly repetitive. Randy begins to understand Adam's problem but still thinks he should be able to manage to get his work done.

Over the next couple of weeks, as Randy continues to see Adam procrastinating, he starts to raise his voice, threatens Adam with "absolutely no going online tonight," and even suggests he might take him off his beloved soccer team (something they both know he would never do). It's time to head off the procrastination.

★ FIRST, TALKING ABOUT IT ★

One Saturday morning, when rain cancels Adam's soccer game, Randy sits down and begins what he hopes to convey will be an open-minded talk.

"Look, kiddo, this thing with the homework is a problem. You seem pretty unhappy this year."

Adam shrugs. "I'll do it. I'll do it," he mumbles. He wants out of this conversation.

"Well, I hope you will do it," Randy says encouragingly. "But I think you need a little help. I understand that a lot of your assignments are a drag."

"No kidding," Adam says sarcastically. He's almost rude, but Randy decides to let it go.

"Last year you liked school a lot. And you were proud of the good grades you earned. This must be a major letdown."

"I can't stand Mr. Friedman." Adam shakes his head. "Do this, do that. It's all the same. Anyway, grades don't matter."

"I can see that grades don't matter that much to you now. And I see how much you don't like the work this year. But I do remember how excited you were last year when you brought home tests and homework with As."

Adam is silent. Randy hopes he's getting in touch with old memories of actually enjoying schoolwork and feeling proud of work well done.

"I don't like it when I have boring work to do either . . ." Randy pauses. "So I try to find a way to get through it so I can get on to doing something I do enjoy."

Adam is silent. He doesn't look convinced.

Randy continues, "Look, I think maybe we can figure out a way for you to be less unhappy about the work you hate. I have a plan that might help you get everything done faster, and then have time to play with your video games and watch a little television. Best of all, I'll stop yelling at you every night! That could make us both happier."

Adam looks at his dad dubiously. "What kind of plan?" he finally asks.

★ THE REWARD PLAN ★

Randy has thought carefully about what kind of incentives and penalties he wants to set. He is concerned that Adam is digging himself into a hole from which he may have difficulty getting out. If he fails to learn school material now, he will be struggling more and more as the year goes on. Randy decides that he should offer both an attractive reward and some penalties for failing to do homework.

Randy knows that Adam is easily distracted by television shows and computer games and that they simply can't be in the picture when it's time for him to work. But they can be offered up when he has completed his responsibilities. It's clear to him that if Adam turns homework in on a particular day, he should be able to enjoy some entertainment activities that evening. However, if he does not turn in homework, he feels it is reasonable to simply restrict those activities for an evening.

In addition, to keep the tone of the program positive, he decides to offer Adam a larger incentive for successfully completing his homework over time. Adam has been asking to take a Saturday computer class for children offered at the local college. Randy thinks this would be a wonderful reward because it would recognize Adam's interest in learning when the subject matter engages him.

Because he realizes that Adam will be upset to hear about the loss of entertainment as a penalty for failing to do homework, Randy decides to first present the reward of the computer class. He tells Adam that he has the opportunity to earn the class he's been begging to take. Adam will be able to sign up for the course if, over the next month, he does his homework regularly. But, he tells Adam, in addition to the opportunity to earn this reward, his plan has another part. Depending on how well he has done the previous day's homework, Adam will either earn or lose privileges to watch television and play computer games that evening.

Randy shows Adam the Privileges chart (for a blank one, see the Pull-Out section at the back of the book) and then lays out the steps of the Reward Plan. He explains to Adam that his "privilege level" for that day will be determined by his performance on his homework the previous evening. He knows that Mr. Friedman reviews homework immediately and fairly and is quite sure he would be willing to give him daily reports. Randy would prefer not to be the homework policeman!

The Privileges chart allows for three levels of achievement and three different degrees of reward. It's quite straightforward, and the judge will be the teacher. Mr. Friedman, in his usual methodical way, always gives four assignments every night. Randy will ask him to indicate how many of the assignments Adam completed. Randy spells out the degrees of reward and their corresponding privileges as follows:

- **Gold Star Level:** Adam has done all his homework. He earns the privilege of one hour of television plus one hour of a video or computer game.
- **Silver Star Level:** Adam has fully done all but one assignment. He earns the privilege of a half hour of television plus a half hour of a video or computer game.
- **Bronze Star Level:** Adam has completely done two assignments. He earns the privilege of a half hour of television or a half hour of a video or computer game.

For Adam to earn the computer classes, he must attain the Gold Star Level at least 10 times during the coming month, and he cannot fall at or below the Bronze Star Level more than 5 days in the next 4 weeks. Randy at first hesitates to give the recognition of Bronze Star Level to Adam for completing only half of his homework, but he decides that because Adam often has not completed any assignments, some acknowledgment of improvement is needed. And Randy knows Adam's stubbornness is going to make it unlikely that he will make a complete turn-around. In any case, the Bronze Star Level limits his evening privileges, plus Randy places a limit of five Bronze Stars for the next month.

Randy can see Adam begin to weigh his options. "You mean I can really take that class?" Adam asks with cautious interest. But then he looks worried. "But I don't know if I can do it!" he moans.

Randy's heart goes out to him, but he knows he's working in the right direction. He's just got to help him figure out some strategies for getting through the tough stuff. "I really do believe we can find some ways to make it easier to get through your homework. Do you have any ideas that would make it less of a pain?"

Adam looks thoughtful. "I get so bored in my room," he begins.

"Do you think you could work better somewhere else?" Randy replies.

Adam frowns and thinks. "How about the kitchen table? Then maybe we could talk a little while I do it. Otherwise, I might pass out from boredom."

After another pause, Adam adds, "And maybe I could do some before dinner and then when you get home, some after."

"Two terrific ideas," Randy answers.

But then Adam, wanting to assert a bit more control over the situation, says, "Weekends don't count, do they? If I mess up on Friday's homework, I can't lose out till Monday evening."

Randy nods. "I wouldn't know until Monday anyway!" he chuckles.

★ WHAT HAPPENS ★

The next evening Adam brings his homework out after dinner. "I saved the most boring part to do with you around," he announces. "I figured I could talk to you while I write these stupid words over and over."

Randy is amazed that Adam is thinking in terms of strategies. And he's even more amazed 40 minutes later when his son announces that he has completed his homework—and after only one short break to play with the dog. Randy is cautiously optimistic that Mr. Friedman, who promised to follow his plan, will validate Adam's success.

The next day, both Randy and Adam are thrilled to find out he's made the Gold Star Level. Adam proudly places a check mark on the chart, then looks over the television schedule and selects two programs. He watches one

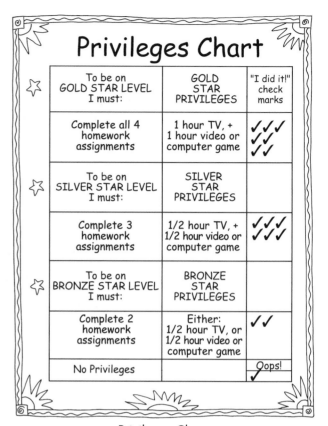

Privileges Chart

	To be on GOLD STAR LEVEL I must:	GOLD STAR PRIVILEGES	"I did it!" check marks
☆	Complete all 4 homework assignments	1 hour TV, + 1 hour video or computer game	✓✓✓ ✓✓✓ ✓✓
☆	To be on SILVER STAR LEVEL I must:	SILVER STAR PRIVILEGES	
	Complete 3 homework assignments	1/2 hour TV, + 1/2 hour video or computer game	✓✓✓ ✓✓✓
☆	To be on BRONZE STAR LEVEL I must:	BRONZE STAR PRIVILEGES	
	Complete 2 homework assignments	Either: 1/2 hour TV, or 1/2 hour video or computer game	✓✓
	No Privileges		Oops! ✓

Privileges Chart

right before dinner, and then after dinner promptly finishes the next day's homework and once again flips on the television. The show is boring, and so he spends an hour on the computer.

Adam works his way through the month, showing much improved homework—most nights achieving on the Gold Star and Silver Star Levels, plus a couple of days that merit the Bronze Star Level. One day when Adam is in a funk, he relapses and does virtually none of his homework. However, because he's fallen at or below the Bronze Star Level only three times, he is still on track for the computer class.

Toward the end of the month, Randy realizes that Adam's work has not met the Gold Star Level quite enough times. He recognizes that failure to earn the computer class could result in Adam's not wanting to try anymore, so he decides to look over his shoulder one day and give him a gentle nudge. "Adam, you only need two more Gold Star Levels. That dictionary page looks kind of incomplete. I think just another few minutes will do the trick." Adam glances up at him, clearly appreciative that he is on his side. His work merits a Gold Star Level the next day. (It is certainly OK to encourage your child and provide the support needed to ensure success. These plans can in many ways be an opportunity for teamwork!)

At the end of the month, Adam is determined to attain his final Gold Star Level check mark. Then a crisis occurs. On the last day of the month, Adam finds himself unable to complete two assignments because he forgot to bring home the worksheets. After searching through his book bag and failing to find the papers, Adam becomes furious at the idea that he will not be able to take the computer class. As he begins shouting that he hates Mr. Friedman and his stupid worksheets, Randy thinks quickly. Adam has improved his homework habits considerably, and he wants him to earn the computer class reward. So he comes up with a way Adam can make up for his mistake of forgetting the papers.

He calms Adam down and tells him he has another chance. If he can complete the two assignments the next day along with the rest of his homework, he will be able to enroll in the class. The next day, Adam manages this feat!

The very next month Adam is proudly enrolled in the computer class, announcing to everyone, "I'm going to college!" Randy notices that his homework is now getting done methodically, and although he misses an assignment occasionally, Adam is tolerating the work and finding ways to deal with the boredom of the tedious assignments. It's clear that Randy has helped Adam get back in touch with the part of himself that wants to be a good student.

★ THE INVISIBLE REWARDS ★

In spite of Adam's claims that he doesn't care about his grades, the next marking period, when his report card comes home with all As and Bs, he asks to bring it over to his grandmother's house on a weekend visit.

Randy's so pleased that the evening struggles with Adam are over. Before the Reward Plan, he had begun to think that Adam had entered adolescence early and that he faced many years of struggle with his growing son. But it turns out that the struggles really were with the hated homework. Randy's relationship with Adam settles down to the comfortable one that preceded his entry into fifth grade. A couple more years of calm and closeness, he hopes, before adolescent turmoil introduces new tensions between the two of them.

And then one night when Randy's fuming about how much he hates bill paying, Adam walks over and suggests that his dad think of something really fun to do when he's finished so he has something fun to look forward to. Adam offers a suggestion. "We could shoot some hoops!"

Adam has learned a very important lesson. It's possible to motivate yourself to do something boring, if you keep in mind there are rewards ahead for getting the job done.

★ ALSO WORKS FOR . . . ★

This kind of Reward Plan works well when you want to recognize and reward responsibilities done at varying levels of either quantity or quality. It could apply to

- chores that can be done sloppily or well;
- weekly progress on long-term assignments;
- music lessons that involve practicing to reach a certain level of performance skill; and
- cooperation with wearing uncomfortable yet necessary items such as a hand splint, eye patch, or orthodontic retainer.

IMPROVING THE QUALITY

Seven-year-old David has just started second grade and for the first time is receiving homework on a daily basis. At open school night, the teacher told parents to expect 20 minutes of homework per evening. But David is getting through his in 10 minutes, and it looks that way, too. His spelling words are barely legible, and on a sheet of 10 math problems, he regularly manages at least four careless errors on the last half. His mother Judy urges him to redo his work, but he angrily asserts, "The teacher thinks it's OK." Judy contacts the teacher and finds out, as she expected, that the teacher has spoken to David several times about the quality of his work and was just about to write Judy a note. Judy asks her to please go ahead and send a note home with David, which she does, and David and Judy promptly read it over together.

He's aggravated. "OK," he says with great annoyance. Very defensively.

Judy hesitates. David is an active boy, and she knows it is hard for him to sit still. She's not sure if his handwriting is poor because he puts so little effort into writing, or whether he puts little effort into it because it is difficult for him. She does know that lots of children at his age have trouble manipulating writing instruments. She suspects he's perfectly capable of addition, because he always gets the first five right, and then once his patience runs out, so do his correct answers.

But whatever is going on, Judy knows she wants to help him strengthen his skills and find ways to get his work done.

★ FIRST, TALKING ABOUT IT ★

The next Monday afternoon, while David is eating his snack, Judy comments that having homework is such a new thing for him. She adds sympathetically that she knows he misses just relaxing in the evening without anything else to do. David averts his eyes and tries to change the subject. He's expecting that she's about to criticize his work.

Judy pushes on. "I have a plan that I think might make getting your homework done *well* a little easier." David sits there with downcast eyes. Suddenly Judy remembers how he used to bring home his drawings in kindergarten. He was so proud. She feels herself melting inside. He's probably, she realizes, feeling awful now . . . and just can't figure out how to make things better.

Judy reminds David that he's been asking for an allowance and suggests that if the two of them could figure out a way for him to spend a little more time getting his work done well, he could start receiving $2 a week.

"I'm doing the best I can!" David wails with tears in his eyes. Judy gives him a hug and assures him she knows he is trying. But she tells him she has some ideas about things he can do differently to get through his homework more easily.

★ THE REWARD PLAN ★

She tells David her plan. She explains that she knows he likes to watch television and play video games, but the rule has been that none of it is allowed until his homework is done. She suggests that maybe it's hard for him to do all his assignments at once, and that might be why things seem to fall apart. "Maybe if you did part of your homework at one time, then played or watched television, and did the rest afterwards, it would be easier for you. You could go back to your video or playtime when everything is done."

As David starts to believe the plan could work,

he's able to focus on the incentive she's offered. "I'm really going to get an allowance?" David asks excitedly.

"Absolutely," Judy replies. "All you have to do is work a little harder on your homework. You need to write more clearly and do all of your math problems carefully."

At this point Judy suggests that David show her his very best writing. She puts his writing homework for the day in front of him and says, "Do the best you can do." She eyes her watch. He labors over the work, and it takes him a full 10 minutes.

"It's not very good," David frowns when he finishes.

It doesn't look beautiful, but it is easy to read, and Judy tells him so. She also tells him that she saw how hard he had to work to write so clearly. "Good for you!" she exclaims. Then she suggests that he write it fast, as if his most favorite show in the world is about to come on and he has to finish. He does so, and again she eyes her wristwatch.

"I can see you save a lot of time when you write fast," she tells David. "I watched the clock, and it took you twice as long to write it really carefully. But it looks so much better!" David looks at the two samples and nods his head.

So now Judy goes about setting up the Reward Plan. She pulls out the Daily Checklist (for a blank one, see the Pull-Out section) and proposes two goals:

1. David begins his writing homework at 6:15 and works until 6:25. Judy will set the kitchen timer to keep track of time spent. David will try to write as clearly as possible.

2. Judy and David play a game together (or he watches television), and then David does the rest of his homework (usually math problems) until he's finished all of them carefully.

If David completes his work in this fashion, he gets a check mark for that day. If he gets a check mark four out of five days, he'll earn a $2 allowance for that week. When he does a poor job, he can choose either to redo his work or to forfeit the check mark. However, each day (beyond the first missed check mark) that he fails to earn a check mark, his allowance will decrease by 50 cents. If David gets a check mark all five days, he can get a 50-cent bonus for the week. Judy will give him his allowance on Saturday morning.

Filled with excitement, David appears hopeful that the new plan will make homework easier. "Can we play cards now?" he asks. "And then I can do the rest of my homework?" Judy agrees immediately, and David enjoys the opportunity to trounce her at Crazy Eights. Then David sits down and moves systematically through each math problem.

As he approaches the last two problems, Judy sees him fidgeting in his chair. She suggests that he get up and stretch. On impulse, she suggests that the two of them play a game of Simon Says for a couple of minutes. He responds enthusiastically to her commands to hop, wave his hands above his head, and do jumping jacks. When he sits back down, he finishes the homework without an error. "Perfect!" Judy announces.

The invisible reward rides again. He loves doing good work.

REMEMBERING THE BOOKS

Eight-year-old Bethany loves her friends. She adores her after-school activities. She cares very much about her schoolwork. But Bethany has one big problem. She is so interested in so many things that when it's time to leave school, that's just what she does. She leaves. She simply cannot seem to remember to stop and think about what she will need that night to do homework assignments. Unfortunately, because she's conscientious, when she gets home and realizes what she's done, she starts crying. She's also a rather high-strung child, and the first few times this happened she was so upset that her mother Vanessa warmly comforted her, shepherded her into the car, and raced to school so that she could retrieve the necessary items.

But it's become a habit now. Bethany walks in the door, and 5 minutes later Vanessa hears, "Mom! I'm sorry! I forgot my World Studies book. We have to go back to school!" Her voice is shrill. She appears at Vanessa's office door, nearly frantic. Only now, Vanessa doesn't feel like warmly comforting her. She's running a business from home, and taking off mid-afternoon to retrieve her daughter's books is getting to be a major pain . . . not to mention of little good to Bethany, who is old enough to remember her own things. "Bethany, this has to stop," Vanessa says sternly as she grabs the car keys. She glances at her daughter, who is now near tears. Vanessa knows she cares about her grades, and she's glad about that. But is it too much to ask that she do what's necessary to complete her own work?

No, it isn't, Vanessa decides. In fact, she realizes, she should expect no less from Bethany. It's just that she obviously needs help.

★ First, Talking About It ★

They're heading into a new week, and on Monday evening Bethany somehow manages to bring home everything she needs for that night's assignments. Vanessa compliments her and notes how much easier it is for both of them when they don't have to chase down her schoolbooks. She nods, eyes downcast. Although Vanessa's tempted to give her an "I see you can do it, so why don't you always do it!" lecture, she stops herself. Bethany's body language is communicating that she feels badly. As Vanessa notices Bethany's shoulders going into a serious slump, she tells her she has a plan to help her work on remembering what to bring home.

★ The Reward Plan ★

"Look, honey," Vanessa begins, as she gives her a hug. "I know you're thinking about a lot of things when you're leaving school. But I have a plan to help make it easier for you to take the time you need to organize yourself." Bethany's shoulders are relaxing, so Vanessa continues. "I know you've been wanting to have a sleepover with Becky and Meredith. But I've been busy, and I guess I've been extra tired with all the trouble we've had with you forgetting stuff. Having two friends over is work for me. I have to get out the air mattress, rearrange your room, and keep your brother away from you and your friends. But if you worked hard on remembering all your homework, books, and papers, I'd be willing to plan for that sleepover."

Bethany's face breaks into a big smile. "Really? When?"

Vanessa makes a deal with her. It's very simple. She explains that if Bethany can bring her assignments and books home every day for a week, she can have a sleepover that weekend. She adds, "I'll have saved up all that energy from not having to drive you back and forth to school, and so I can spend it on planning for your company!"

"Oh, wow!" Bethany exclaims. "And I've already done it today, so only 4 more days, and I can have a sleepover this weekend!"

"Yes, Bethany," Vanessa replies with a serious tone in her voice. "But remember. It's not like you've wanted to leave your things behind. I know you haven't. I think we're going to have to come up with a few ways for you to remind yourself to bring everything you need home."

Bethany immediately explains that what happens after school is that she starts talking to her friends, and pretty soon she's just following them out the door without a thought in her head. Vanessa nods with understanding and then suggests that the two of them come up with some creative ideas to help her remember. If one idea doesn't work, another one is bound to. Here's what they decide:

- Before Bethany leaves for school, she will write the word *sleepover* in the palm of her hand. She'll undoubtedly notice it throughout the day.
- Bethany will attach a tiny bell (she has one on an old bracelet she never wears) to the spiral binding of her assignment book. It will help her to remember to write everything down. It will also undoubtedly jingle as

she sprints out the front doors of school, further reminding her to think.

- Bethany will ask one of her friends to be a "helper." It will be that friend's job to check on Bethany. As they near the school door, she will whisper, "Bethany, have you got everything?"

Bethany and Vanessa agree to keep track of her success on the kitchen calendar using a purple pen. Each time she arrives home with everything she needs, Bethany writes a big R on the date (for *remembered*!).

"Maybe I should also wear a purple shirt tomorrow to help me remember!" Bethany says.

Vanessa agrees, and that night as she tucks her daughter in, she says, "From now on, we're going to say a little mantra before you go to sleep. You know, a kind of chant." Vanessa grins. Then she closes her eyes and says, twice, "Books home . . . books home . . ."

Bethany laughs, saying it once herself with her eyes closed.

★ WHAT HAPPENS ★

The next day, Bethany arrives home with everything. "My friend forgot to say a word, and I didn't think a second about my purple shirt!" she announced. "I heard the bell a few times and got most stuff written down. But do you know what really did it? I opened my hand at the end of the day to take a mint from a friend, and there it was, *sleepover*! I realized I'd forgotten my geography notebook!"

"Well," Vanessa says, "That's the beauty of a backup system. If one thing doesn't work, something else will."

Bethany just about never forgets her work anymore. She's calm as she does her work and clearly feels happy to be in charge. Vanessa is not missing any important business calls, and the only problem now is that Bethany's brother wants sleepovers, too. Bethany agrees to trade off weekends, even though she's bringing everything home. It doesn't seem to occur to her that she "deserves" anything every week for packing up her work and bringing it home. That's the clearest sign that a Reward Plan has been a genuine success.

Your Toolbox: Reward Charts and More

Introduction

Time for action!

By now you probably have a clear idea about what behavior problems you want to tackle, and what kinds of incentives your child needs for motivation. All that remains is choosing the right chart, setting it up, and getting it going.

Part 3 includes a large variety of charts from which to choose. Each chart is described in chapter 11 along with an example of it in use. Then, the Pull-Out section that follows chapter 11 includes the ready-to-use charts and reward items to remove when you want to get started!

An easy way to begin would probably be with one of the *Basic Charts for Tracking Progress*. These include the Design-Your-Own chart (best for ages 3–8) and the Keeping Track and Daily Checklist charts (best for ages 6–10).

If you have children ages 3–6, another good place to start would be with one of the *My-Own-Picture Charts*. Here, the chart is the reward; all you need do is purchase stickers appropriate for the chart's contents. Virtually all young children will be excited about at least one of these charts, which include Welcome to the Zoo, Dinosaur Land, Playhouse, and Feed the Kitty.

If your goal is to track progress, and you want a chart that is a little more imaginative but also a bit more work, look at the *Tracking With an Imaginative Twist* charts. The Treasure Hunt chart and Pockets for Points chart work best for ages 4–7. The Blue Lagoon chart is best for ages 5–8, and the Privileges chart is best for ages 7–10.

Finally, there are *All the Extras*, such as novel awards, certificates, and contracts. Children ages 3–6 may enjoy the Happy Tokens, Gold Medals, Picture Contract, and "I Did It!" Certificates. For ages 4–7, use Prize Coupons, Activity Treats, Tickets, and "I Made a Mistake!" Slips. The Contract is useful for children with some reading skills, usually age 6 and up.

Before you begin using a chart, consider whether you should make a copy for future use. Will a new chart be needed every week for a reward plan likely to last several weeks? Will your younger child clamor for his own chart? In 6 months, will you want to use the same chart to tackle a new behavior problem?

Try to involve your child in the chart's creation whenever possible. If your daughter loves to draw or color, offer her the opportunity to decorate one of the charts or reward items that invites coloring, such as a Design-Your-Own chart, Happy Token, or Prize Coupon. Less artistically oriented children can apply decorative stickers or enjoy having you attach their photo to charts or awards. If you or your child particularly enjoys arts and crafts projects, you may even want to get out the glitter glue, sequins, and ribbons and come up with a one-of-a-kind creation together!

But if you're a busy parent, you shouldn't feel pressure to spend time creating an extra special chart. Children will be happy with the charts and awards with simple or no modifications. Don't allow the wish to create the perfect chart delay you from implementing your Reward Plan. It's time to get going!

CHAPTER ELEVEN

Guide to the Charts and Activities

In this chapter I'll be explaining in more detail how to select and use a chart that works for your child. There are four main categories: Basic Charts for Tracking Progress, My-Own-Picture Charts, Tracking With an Imaginative Twist, and All the Extras.

BASIC CHARTS FOR TRACKING PROGRESS

The three kinds of Basic Charts are easy to use, simple to prepare, and provide a straightforward way of keeping track of your child's successes. The Design-Your-Own chart appeals to younger children who may want to personalize their chart. The Keeping Track and Daily Checklist charts are best for older children who simply need a place to record their progress. These charts are very flexible and can be used in all kinds of ways, limited only by your creativity. You can find the Basic Charts in the Pull-Out section that follows this chapter. The Design-Your-Own chart, however, is larger and can be found folded at the back of the book.

★ DESIGN-YOUR-OWN CHART ★

The blank spaces on this chart can be used in many different ways. For example, consider the four rectangular spaces forming a column at the left side of the chart. They can be used to list separate behavior goals, as seen in Latisha's chart.

Or, if the chart will be used to track progress towards a single goal over several weeks, these rectangular spaces can be used to record weeks number 1, 2, 3, and 4, as illustrated by Tyler's chart in chapter 1 (p. 9). Another option is to design this to be a family chart, putting each family member's name and goal in one space in the left-hand column. A family chore chart can be found in chapter 9 (p. 99).

The row of "heading" boxes running across the top of the chart can also be used in different ways. If you list the 7 days of the week in this row, there are two spaces left for totaling points or check marks earned over the week, if that fits with your Reward Plan. Or, the heading boxes can be left blank, and you can just fill the grid of boxes below them with check marks, stars, or stickers accrued many times daily. Each box in the grid can hold a single star or check mark, or a number of check marks and stars can be placed in each box.

This chart can be adapted to tally misbehaviors that earn penalty points in addition to recording instances of desired behaviors. Just place stickers, check marks, or X's on a separate line, as shown in the example on the right, which uses sketches of happy and sad faces to help a young child understand how good and bad behaviors are being recorded.

Finally, be sure to add some inspiring title, photo, or pictures at the top of the chart or hanging around its edges!

Additional examples of the Design-Your-Own chart in use can be found in chapter 3 and with Rebecca and Steven in chapter 5.

Design-Your-Own Chart

Design-Your-Own Chart

★KEEPING TRACK CHART★

The Keeping Track chart has three columns that can be used in whatever way you please. Provide each column with a label, perhaps "Date" followed by one or two goals, or use separate columns to record instances of positive and negative behaviors. The chart is designed to offer maximum flexibility. In the examples shown below, Eric (see chapter 6) receives check marks if he remains on schedule to be in bed by 10:15 p.m., and Matthew (see chapter 4) works to avoid pushing his friends and to develop more positive ways of relating. More ways of using the Keeping Track charts can be found in the sample Reward Plans with Kendra in chapter 5 and with Melissa and Karen in chapter 8.

Keeping Track

	8:30 PM PREPARE FOR SCHOOL PLAY CHECKERS	9:15 PM PREPARE FOR BED	9:45 PM RELAX 10:15 LIGHTS OUT
Mon 4/1		✓	✓
Tues 4/2	✓		✓
Wed 4/3	✓	✓	✓
Thur 4/4		✓	✓
Fri 4/5			
Mon 4/8			
Tues 4/9			
Wed 4/10			
Thur 4/11			
Fri 4/12			

Keeping Track

I Did It!	I Goofed	Date
✓✓✓✓		Sat 6/1 ✓
✓✓✓✓	✓✓	Sun 6/9 ✗
✓✓	✓	Sat 6/15 ✓
✓✓✓	✓	Fri 6/21 ✓
✓		Sat 6/22 ✓
✓✓		Sun 6/30 ✓

Keeping Track Charts

★DAILY CHECKLIST CHART★

The Daily Checklist chart can also be used in a variety of ways. Successful completion of chores, tasks, or activities that must be performed once or more daily can be recorded by placing check marks or stars on the chart.

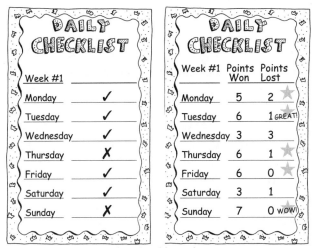

DAILY CHECKLIST

Week #1	
Monday	✓
Tuesday	✓
Wednesday	✓
Thursday	✗
Friday	✓
Saturday	✓
Sunday	✗

DAILY CHECKLIST

Week #1	Points Won	Points Lost	
Monday	5	2	★
Tuesday	6	1	GREAT!
Wednesday	3	3	
Thursday	6	1	★
Friday	6	0	★
Saturday	3	1	
Sunday	7	0	WOW!

Daily Checklist Charts

You can also pair the Daily Checklist with the Pockets for Points chart (p. 125) or with Tickets or Mistake Slips (p. 129) to keep track of the number of Points, Tickets, or Slips earned each day.

More examples of using the Daily Checklist chart can be found in the sample Reward Plans with Elisa in chapter 7, Katie in chapter 8 (shown above on the right), and David in chapter 10.

MY-OWN-PICTURE CHARTS

The My-Own-Picture charts—Welcome to the Zoo, Dinosaur Land, Playhouse and Feed the Kitty—offer the modest reward of a sticker, yet they still entertain and capture the imaginations of younger children. It's a treat for children to choose a sticker, decide on its placement, and create an attractive picture. These activities also give children a feeling of independence and control, even though they are complying with your demands!

★GETTING READY★

You'll need to buy stickers appropriate for the chart you've chosen to use. Stickers can easily be found in toy and drug stores as well as in many art and hobby shops. Zoo animals, dinosaurs, and food and household items are readily available. With the Playhouse chart, you can use your imagination in finding a set of family figures. If you don't locate human figures, you might choose animal ones, or use paper doll cut-outs or figures from a magazine. You can find the Feed the Kitty chart in the Pull-Out section that follows this chapter. The Welcome to the Zoo, Dinosaur Land, and Playhouse charts are larger and can be found folded at the back of the book.

★ How to Use The Picture Charts ★

Simply award a sticker to your child each time she behaves in the desired way. To increase your child's interest, you can encourage her to color the chart, give names to the characters or animals, and eventually hang the chart in her room, in the playroom, or on the kitchen fridge where she can enjoy her creation. Take a peek at the examples to the right.

More examples of the My-Own-Picture charts in use can be found in the sample Reward Plans with Alex in chapter 4, Carlos in chapter 6, Sara in chapter 7, and Christy in chapter 9.

Feed the Kitty Chart

TRACKING WITH AN IMAGINATIVE TWIST

You've done a few Basic Charts, and your daughter's eyes no longer sparkle when you suggest a new Reward Plan. Or you're looking for an attention-grabbing chart that your son will find irresistible, despite his stubborn determination not to change his behavior. Or maybe you are simply the kind of parent who from the start likes to try something a bit more complicated but also a little more creative.

Playhouse Chart

The charts that follow require somewhat more thought and preparation than the Basic Charts. But the effort may be well worth it if the chart holds your child's attention!

★ Treasure Hunt Chart ★

Searching for treasures is a reward in itself! The Treasure Hunt chart rewards your child by guiding her as she advances each step after a good behavior, follows a clue, and finds a hidden reward. The sense of adventure makes the hidden "treasure" more exciting than it would be if you just handed it over.

Getting Ready
Before starting, you must collect a variety of prizes for your child to find. Use your imagination: stickers, inexpensive toys, Prize Coupons (see Pull-Out

section) for outings or activities, favorite cookies, attractively wrapped pieces of candy, or nickels or dimes are all possibilities. Then remove the Treasure Hunt chart—it is one of the larger charts that can be found folded at the back of the book.

Treasure Hunt Chart

Using the Chart

Each time your child earns the opportunity to advance one step on the Treasure Hunt chart, he can search for a treasure following the clue on the chart. Be sure to keep track of your child's progress and hide each treasure ahead of time. That way, there will always be a piece of loot to find as he gets to solve the next clue.

If your child has difficulty locating the prize, be generous with hints; the object is for her to feel that she is a successful sleuth! After your child has found the treasure, place an X on that step.

You can find a sample Reward Plan using this chart with Heather in chapter 6.

★ POCKETS FOR POINTS CHART ★

Pockets for Points charts are great for children who love doing things themselves. The points are slips of paper that are moved into pockets after your child behaves in a way that you are either encouraging or discouraging. The chart needs to be assembled by taping the three pockets to the chart background; once assembled, this chart can be reused. The chart can be found in the Pull-Out section that follows this chapter.

Getting Ready

To assemble a Pockets for Points chart, follow these seven simple steps:

1. Remove the Pockets for Points chart (2 pages) from the Pull-Out section as well as the Sun and Cloud Point Slips sheet.
2. Cut out the three pockets (the Sun, the Cloud, and the Rainbow) along the solid outer lines. (Do NOT cut out the backs of the pockets that appear on the chart page!)
3. Place the cut-out pockets over the corresponding

Pockets for Points Chart

numbered designs on the chart, and secure them in place by matching up the diagonal lines on three sides of each pocket with tape.

4. If you want, invite your child to color the Pockets for Points chart and Sun and Cloud Point Slips.
5. Cut out the Sun and Cloud Point Slips.
6. Write your child's name in the box in the Point Keeper's pocket at the bottom of the page.
7. Place the Point Slips in the Point Keeper's pocket at the bottom of the chart.

Using the Chart

Each time your child earns a point, he can take a Sun Point from the Point Keeper's pocket and place it in the Points Won! pocket. When he loses a point, he takes a Cloud Point from the Point Keeper's pocket and places it in the Points Lost pocket.

Reward your child for earning a certain number of Sun Points without getting more than a specified number of Cloud Points. Your child could earn a small reward each day, or she could earn a reward after meeting minimum point goals for a number of days. If your child must work for several days to earn the reward, you can use the Daily Checklist to record points earned and lost.

A sample Reward Plan using the Pockets for Points chart can be found with Katie in chapter 8.

★ BLUE LAGOON CHART ★

The Blue Lagoon chart is a creative way to keep track of desired and undesired behaviors, and the innovative format can help inspire children to strive for good behavior. With the Blue Lagoon chart (which is a larger chart that can be found folded at the back of the book), two rafts sail to their destinations. One raft, called *Ocean Breeze*, is propelled forward by good behaviors, and the second, *Ragged Raft*, gets its power from misbehaviors. Obviously, the goal is for *Ocean Breeze* to win!

The rafts follow two routes with different end points; *Ocean Breeze* heads for the idyllic Blue Lagoon, and *Ragged Raft* ends up in the Dismal

Swamp. The path to the Blue Lagoon is longer than the path to the Swamp because it gives your children more opportunities to move *Ocean Breeze* forward by engaging in positive behaviors than to move *Ragged Raft* because of negative behaviors. Thus, the emphasis stays on good behavior!

The Blue Lagoon chart is suitable either for an individual child or for teams of two or more children working together. When you set up a Reward Plan for a team of children, the aim is to encourage a cooperative spirit. You can stipulate that *Ocean Breeze* will move forward if any one of the children performs a desired behavior. Likewise, the misbehaviors of any one child will propel *Ragged Raft* forward.

I do not recommend that you use the two routes to separately record the accomplishments of two children. Particularly with siblings, setting up a situation where there will be a loser as well as a winner is bound to lead to hurt feelings.

Getting Ready

In deciding on the list of behaviors that will move the rafts forward, you should consider the relative lengths of the two routes. There are 30 spaces on the Blue Lagoon route and 12 spaces on the Swamp route. Thus, for the rafts to race neck and neck, your child must perform two or three good behaviors for every misbehavior. If you expect your child to misbehave more often, you can simply add more spaces to the Swamp route by dividing single spaces into two spaces

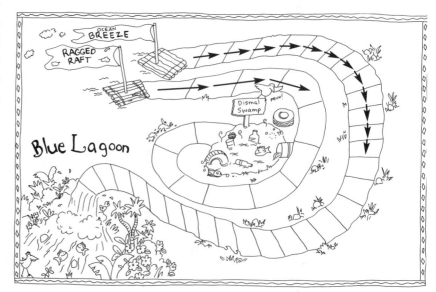

Blue Lagoon Chart

with a black pen. You certainly want your child to be successful, so be sure that the list of behaviors needed to move *Ocean Breeze* is generous enough for it to keep ahead! Finally, decide on a reward to be earned . . . assuming *Ocean Breeze* wins.

Using the Blue Lagoon Chart
Every time a child performs one of the designated behaviors, indicate the appropriate raft's progress by drawing an arrow through each step on the route with a bright marker or pencil.

You can find a sample Reward Plan using this chart with Pat and Chris in chapter 8.

★ PRIVILEGES CHART ★

If you're trying to help your older child improve the quality of his work in one area or another, the Privileges chart may be a good choice. It helps you reward varying levels of work quality by tying daily privileges to the quality of, for example, a night's homework or a week's musical instrument practice. Or, you may want to reward varying degrees of cooperation with a prescribed medical program, such as wearing a hand splint or an eye patch. In addition, you can track progress toward a larger reward, which will be earned after a specific amount of time.

Getting Ready
You need to think carefully about what level of quality or degree of cooperation you can realistically expect and about how you will evaluate the success of your child's efforts. You may want to ask your child's teacher or music instructor whether she would be willing to rate your child's work on a regular basis. Or perhaps the amount of time spent on homework or practicing can provide the yardstick you need. If the goal is compliance with a medical program, you might rely on the report of an observer, such as the classroom teacher, or if your child is at home you could set up a system of spot checks.

You also should think about the privileges your child will earn at each level of work quality or degree of cooperation. If you decide to establish your child's current set of privileges as the Gold Star Level, and your child rarely performs at the Gold Star Level now, he may see the lesser privileges of the Silver Star and Bronze Star Levels as punishment. To sweeten the tone of the plan, you could offer an end-of-plan reward for showing improvement over time. If you offer an extra reward, decide on the minimum number of check marks needed at the various levels to earn the reward. (For example, for a reward plan that will last 2 weeks, you might require your child to attain Gold Star Level at least 7 days and not fall at or below Bronze Star Level

Privileges Chart

To be on GOLD STAR LEVEL I must:	GOLD STAR PRIVILEGES	"I did it!" check marks
Wear hand splint at least 10 hours / day	- Get ride to school next day. - Hot lunch at school next day. - Favorite dessert for dinner.	✓✓
To be on SILVER STAR LEVEL I must:	SILVER STAR PRIVILEGES	
Wear hand splint at least 8 hours / day	- Hot lunch at school next day. - Favorite dessert for dinner.	✓✓
To be on BRONZE STAR LEVEL I must:	BRONZE STAR PRIVILEGES	
Wear hand splint at least 6 hours / day	- Hot lunch at school next day.	✓
No Privileges	Wear splint less than 6 hours / day	Oops! ✓

Privileges Chart

more than twice.)

Alternatively, the Gold Star Level can offer your child privileges she doesn't currently have. Then no extra reward need be offered; the reward is the expanded set of privileges, which she can enjoy as long as she meets the goal.

Using the Privileges Chart

Fill out the chart with agreed on behaviors and privileges. Place a check mark in the "I did it!" column every time your child performs the behavior required to meet the Gold, Silver, or Bronze Levels. Strive to keep the tone of the plan positive! If your child loses privileges, sympathize and look for ways to help him find opportunities to regain them.

A sample Reward Plan using this chart can be found with Adam in chapter 10.

ALL THE EXTRAS

Included in this section are an array of items which can either add variety to a Reward Plan or can provide a formal way of starting or ending a plan. You can use a Contract (p. 130) to clearly state the terms of the plan before you begin, and then an "I Did It!" Certificate (p. 131) to mark the conclusion of the plan. Here you'll also find unusual reward items that appeal to young children, such as Happy Tokens and Activity Treats, which can provide very simple yet motivating rewards.

★ HAPPY TOKENS, GOLD MEDALS, AND PRIZE COUPONS ★

Young children can be pleased with a simple paper item providing recognition of a job well done. Happy Tokens and Gold Medals are a reward in themselves; you need not promise anything more than these special pieces of paper. Prize Coupons help make a small prize or activity earned all the more special. Plus, being able to hold the slip of paper helps young children wait for a reward to be delivered at a later time.

Remove the appropriate page from the Pull-Out section that follows this chapter, make some photocopies if you anticipate this item may be a big hit with your child, and cut out the tokens, medals or coupons. Then write an appropriate phrase on them, and perhaps draw a picture to communicate the action being rewarded or the activity being promised. For example, if a Happy Token is awarded for cooperation in taking medication, you might write on the back of it "I took my medicine like a big girl!" (Even though your daughter may not be able to read, your enthusiastic recital of the words as you write them should please your child.) Or, if a Gold Medal is awarded after your son has avoided pushing his younger brother for one or more days, you might draw a sketch of your two children arm-in-arm and then write "First Prize for being a good big brother!" Prize Coupons offer the promise of a reward to be delivered later, so you might inscribe on them

Happy Token, Gold Medal, and Prize Coupon

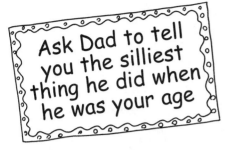

Ask Dad to tell you the silliest thing he did when he was your age

Get a ribbon braid in your hair

Choose tomorrow night's dinner (from menu provided)

Activity Treats

I Made A Mistake!

Tickets and Mistake Slips

"We'll bake cookies together!" or "I have earned 1 trip to the park."

You or your child can decorate these items with stickers, markers, glitter glue, or pieces of yard or ribbon. You might want to give your child a special box, such as a shoe box covered with wrapping paper, in which to keep the tokens or coupons. The Gold Medals can be glued to a piece of cardboard to prevent tearing, strung with ribbon, and then proudly worn by the recipient!

A sample Reward Plan using Happy Tokens is demonstrated with Sara in chapter 7, a plan using a Gold Medal appears with Alex in chapter 4, and a plan using Prize Coupons is found with Sally in the Party Departure Plan in chapter 1.

★ ACTIVITY TREATS ★

Here's an easy way to make out-of-the-ordinary activities into special rewards: Your child reaches into a container, pulls out a slip of paper describing an activity, and gets to enjoy the Activity Treat. The surprise is part of the fun!

Activity Treats can be found at the back of the book with some suggested activities. Choose the treats you think would most interest your child, or come up with your own ideas and write them on the forms. Then, place the Activity Treats in a colorful paper bag or other container. When your child performs in the desired way, let him reach into the bag and pull out the reward!

You can find a sample Reward Plan using Activity Treats with Sara in chapter 7.

★ TICKETS AND MISTAKE SLIPS ★

Rather than recording points on a chart, you can acknowledge your child's behavior in a more concrete way by handing your child a Ticket when she succeeds in meeting a goal or an "I Made a Mistake!" Slip when a misbehavior occurs. Young children enjoy holding and counting Tickets, which can help them feel in charge of the Reward Plan. The Mistake Slips provide a fairly neutral way to communicate to your child that he has made a mistake.

You can use the Tickets as they are, or your child can color them with crayons, markers, or watercolors. If he wants to color the tickets, it may be easier to do so before they are cut apart. Then, after you've cut them out along the solid lines, store them in a container such as an envelope or special pouch, and provide a separate container for your child to keep the Tickets he earns. A coffee can covered with paper (wrapping paper or plain paper decorated by your child) is a great "Ticket Bank" to hold Tickets earned; just cut a slit in the plastic lid.

In most cases, Tickets and Mistake Slips form part of Reward Plans that promise a reward for a certain number of Tickets earned or a penalty for Mistake Slips acquired. (You might want to keep a separate record of the Tickets and Mistake Slips given so that none disappear!) Sometimes, though,

Contract

Picture Contract

children find the recognition provided by Tickets and the warning given by Mistake Slips sufficient in themselves to change in the desired direction.

A sample Reward Plan using Tickets is shown with Lauren in chapter 1; a plan using Mistake Slips is shown with Ebony also in chapter 1.

★ CONTRACT ★

A Contract can be useful for many reasons. For one thing, it underlines the seriousness of the Reward Plan. The "grown-up" feel of such an agreement can also be flattering: "Wow—Dad really thinks I'm old enough to sign a Contract!" And there's no denying that they make the terms of the plan clear to all.

Discuss the terms of the Contract with your child, making clear what you require and when the requirements must be met. If your child suggests reasonable modifications, accept them: That's what negotiation is all about! Then fill out the Contract and join with your child in signing the document.

You can find sample Reward Plans using Contracts with Elisa in chapter 7 and Paul in chapter 9.

★ PICTURE CONTRACT ★

Just because your young child does not yet read or write doesn't mean she can't "sign" an agreement! You can describe a deal using pictures, and a Picture Contract can both provide a visual reminder of the Reward Plan and intrigue your young child. In addition, a Picture Contract can be used to help your child understand the time frame for a reward to be earned. You can see in the example above (based on the sample Reward Plan for Carlos in chapter 6) that the seven circles represent the seven days Carlos must sleep in his own bed before earning a trip to the zoo.

With young children, negotiation of the terms of the contract is less helpful than with older ones. Younger children expect their parents to tell them what's what. So go ahead and draw pictures showing some aspect of the desired behavior in the upper section (labeled Me!) and of the promised reward in the lower section (labeled You!). Add captions, if you wish. When you present it to your child, he can "sign" by coloring or decorating the chart.

Simply post the contract in a prominent location and be ready to come through with your end of the deal when your child makes good on hers!

★ "I Did It!" Certificate ★

The final touch! An "I Did It!" Certificate provides one more way to congratulate your child for a job well done. It also carries the message that the Reward Plan is over and that you expect your child to continue with the improved behavior without any further reward.

When a Reward Plan has come to an end and your child has shown significant improvement over its course, fill out one of these certificates and award it proudly to him. If you and your child enjoy a little drama, you might stage a reward ceremony during which you make a formal announcement of his achievement, and then present the certificate. If you're planning another Reward Plan aimed at a different behavior problem, you can provide your child with a cardboard box to decorate and use for storing all his certificates. Hopefully, your child will aspire for a collection of them!

You can find a sample Reward Plan using an "I Did It!" Certificate with Heather in chapter 6.

"I Did It!" Certificate

Pull-Out Charts,
Awards, Contracts,
and Extras

☺ Keeping Track ☺

_____ _____ _____
_____ _____ _____
_____ _____ _____
_____ _____ _____
_____ _____ _____
_____ _____ _____
_____ _____ _____
_____ _____ _____

- CUT HERE - - - ✂

☺ Keeping Track ☺

_____ _____ _____
_____ _____ _____
_____ _____ _____
_____ _____ _____
_____ _____ _____
_____ _____ _____
_____ _____ _____
_____ _____ _____

DAILY CHECKLIST

CUT HERE

DAILY CHECKLIST

CHART

1

TAPE POCKET FRONT ON
2 SIDES AND BOTTOM

2

TAPE POCKET FRONT ON
2 SIDES AND BOTTOM

3

TAPE POCKET FRONT ON
2 SIDES AND BOTTOM

Pockets for Points

Pockets For Points

POINTS WON!

CUT OUT
AND TAPE
TO #1
TO MAKE
A POCKET

POINTS LOST

CUT OUT
AND TAPE
TO #2
TO MAKE
A POCKET

'S

POINT KEEPER'S POCKET

CUT OUT
AND TAPE
TO #3
TO MAKE
A POCKET

POINT SLIPS

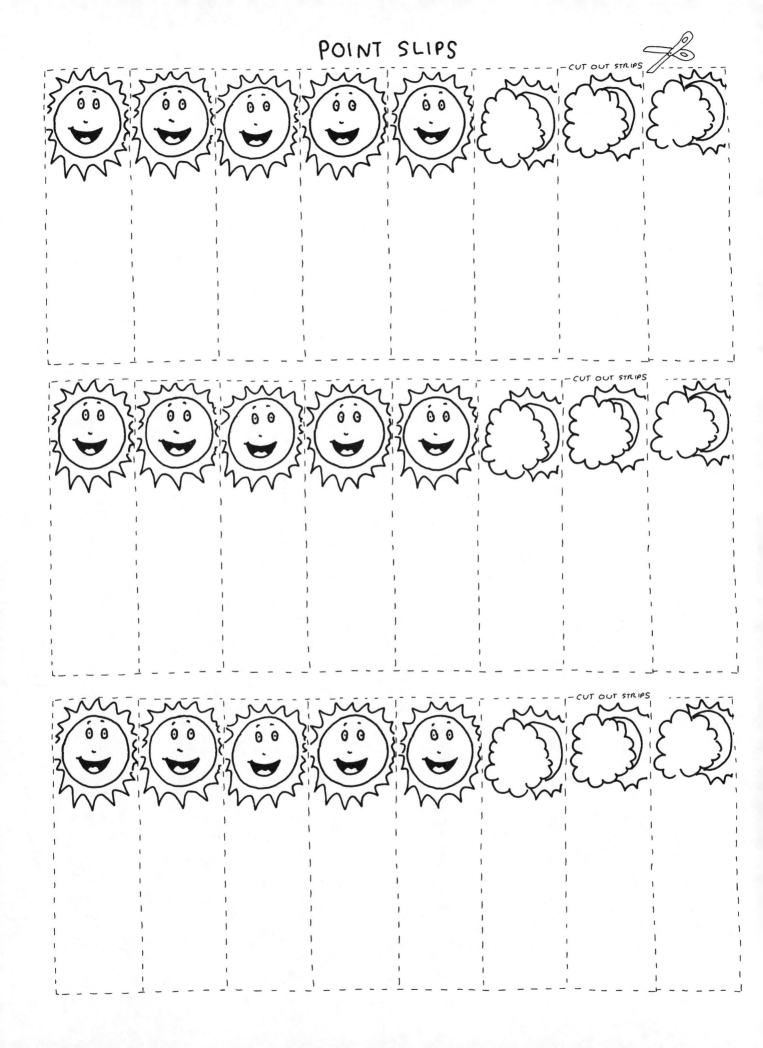

CUT OUT STRIPS

CUT OUT STRIPS

CUT OUT STRIPS

Privileges Chart

To be on GOLD STAR LEVEL I must:	GOLD STAR PRIVILEGES	"I did it!" check marks
To be on SILVER STAR LEVEL I must:	SILVER STAR PRIVILEGES	
To be on BRONZE STAR LEVEL I must:	BRONZE STAR PRIVILEGES	
No Privileges		Oops!

CUT OUT TOKENS

CUT HERE

HAPPY TOKENS!

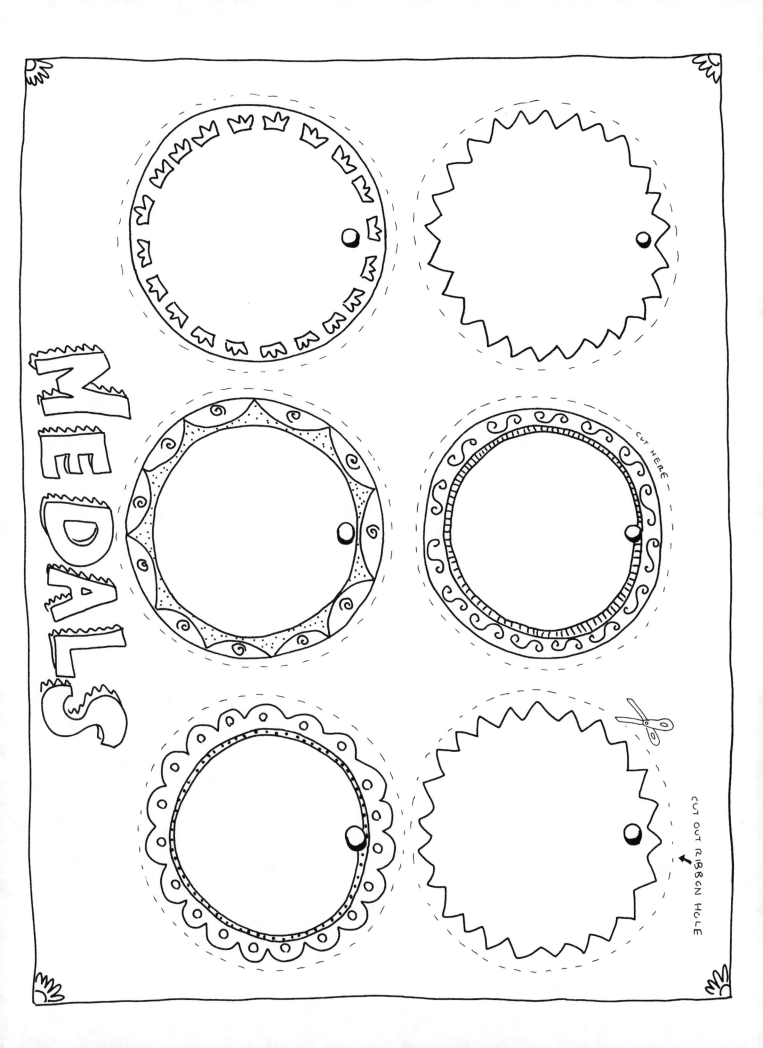

MEDALS

CUT HERE

CUT OUT RIBBON HOLE

Prize Coupon
I have earned:

Prize Coupon
I have earned:

PRIZE COUPON
I have earned:

PRIZE COUPON
I have earned:

Prize Coupon!

Prize Coupon!

Prize Coupon!

Prize Coupon!

PRIZE COUPON!

PRIZE COUPON!

Activity Treats

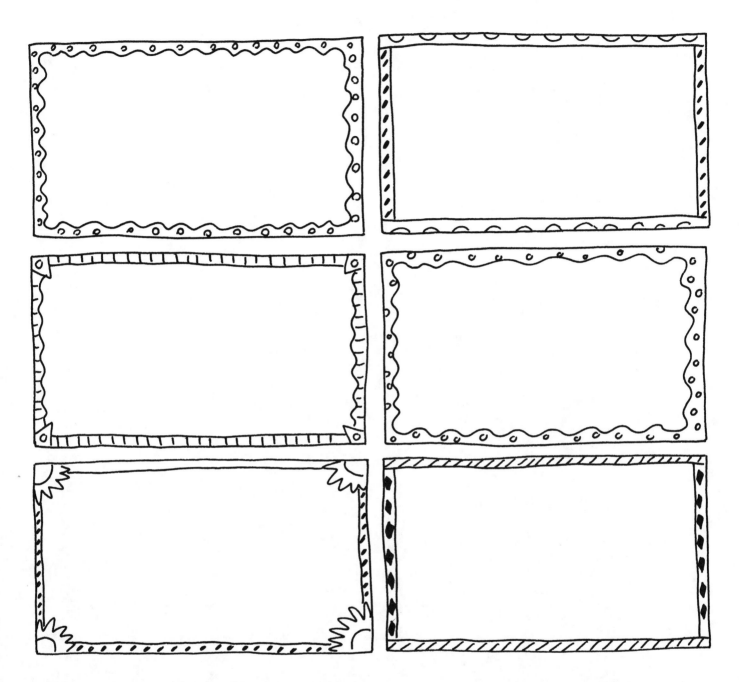

Fill in the blank slips above with activities your child will enjoy. Here are some suggestions:

Choose tomorrow night's dinner (from menu provided)

Ask Mom to sing her favorite song

Get a piggy-back ride

Make a puzzle

Make pudding with Mom or Dad

Get a ribbon braid in your hair

Have a car race with Mom or Dad

Make a paper airplane

Build a block castle with Mom or Dad

Make a heart necklace with string and paper

Learn a new dance

Tickets

CUT OUT TICKETS

Picture
CONTRACT

Me!
(CHILD)

You!
(ADULT)

I DID IT!
CERTIFICATE

I DID IT!
CERTIFICATE

CUT HERE

I DID IT!
CERTIFICATE

CUT HERE

Contract

Signed _____

Signed _____

Date _____

- - - CUT HERE - - - - - - -

Contract

Signed _____

Signed _____

Date _____

Design-Your-Own Chart

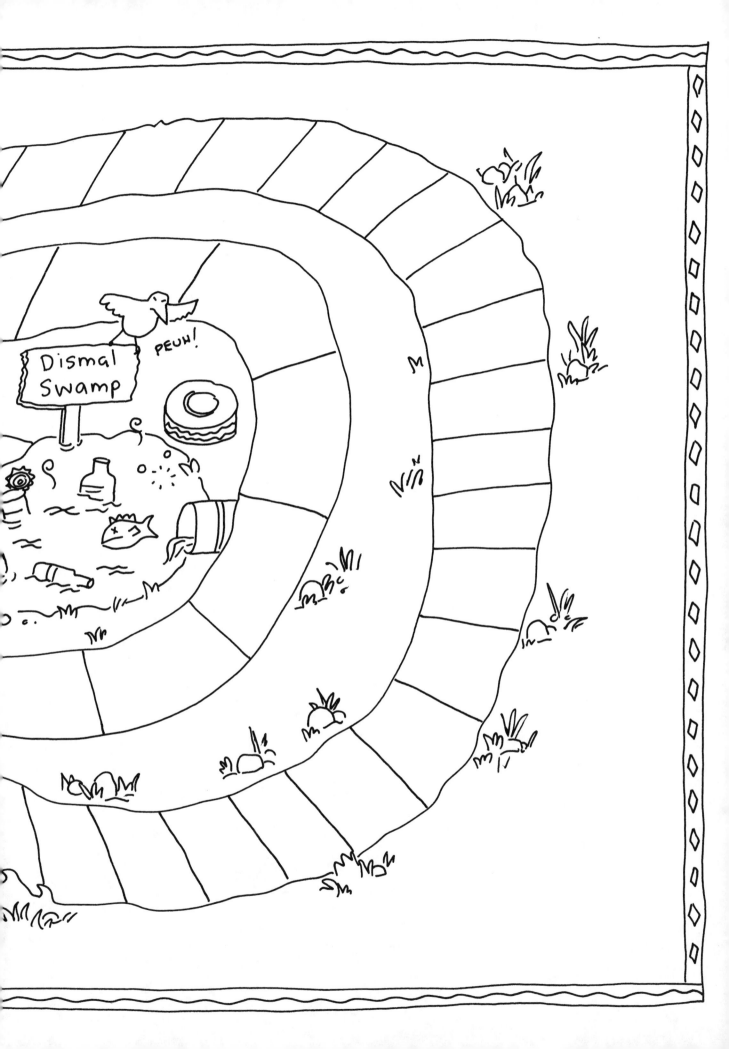

PLAY HOUSE

Land